ISTANBUL

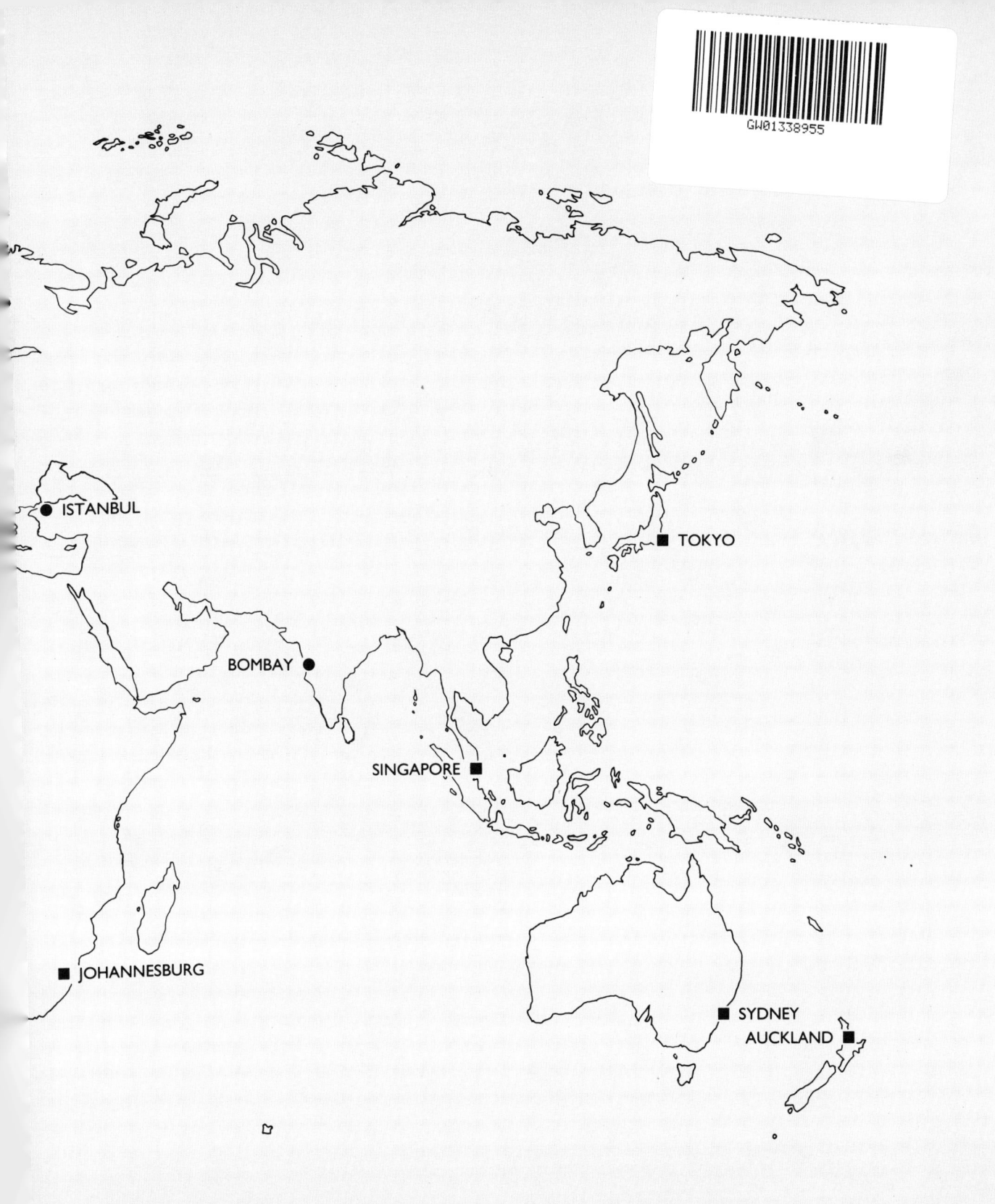

TOKYO

BOMBAY

SINGAPORE

JOHANNESBURG

SYDNEY
AUCKLAND

● REPRESENTATIVE OFFICES

GREIG FESTER
A Story of Reinsurance

GREIG FESTER

GREIG FESTER
A Story of Reinsurance

Antony Brown

GRANTA EDITIONS

© 1996 Greig Fester Group Limited
Devon House, 58–60 St Katharine's Way, London E1 9LB, UK

Published by Granta Editions,
25–27 High Street, Chesterton, Cambridge CB4 1ND, UK

*Granta Editions is a wholly owned imprint of
Book Production Consultants plc*

All rights reserved. No part of this publication may be
reproduced, stored in a retrieval system or transmitted in any
form or by any means, electronic, mechanical, photocopying,
recording or otherwise, without the prior written permission of
the copyright holder for which application should be addressed
in the first instance to the publishers. No liability shall be
attached to the author, the copyright holder or the publishers
for loss or damage of any nature suffered as a result of reliance
on the reproduction of any of the contents of this publication
or any errors or omissions in its contents.

A CIP catalogue record for this book is available
from the British Library.

ISBN 1 85757 033 2

Designed by Peter Dolton
Text typeset in Monotype Ehrhardt 11/14½ pt
Printed by Proost N.V. in Belgium
Produced in association with Book Production Consultants plc
25–27 High Street, Chesterton, Cambridge CB4 1ND, UK

Contents

FOREWORD	*1*
INTRODUCTION	*3*
CHAPTER ONE *Early days*	*5*
CHAPTER TWO *Festers and the European scene*	*23*
CHAPTER THREE *Honeymoon*	*35*
CHAPTER FOUR *The inter-war years*	*47*
CHAPTER FIVE *Innovation and change*	*59*
CHAPTER SIX *Two and two make five*	*79*
CHAPTER SEVEN *Today's professionals*	*95*
GLOSSARY	*111*
FURTHER READING	*113*
ACKNOWLEDGEMENTS	*115*
INDEX	*117*

Foreword

Whilst it is 75 years since Walter Greig and his brothers drove into Nicholas Lane to accept the exciting challenge of starting a new company in those difficult post-war years, the roots of Greig Fester go further back in time. The year of 1874, more than 120 years ago, marks the beginning of our story for it was then that our Fester forebears established the foundations of a business based on integrity, professionalism and service.

By City standards 120 years is a solid apprenticeship and one which deserves to be appropriately recorded. Furthermore, we were concerned at the risk in our modern world of mislaying the archives which bear witness to much of our history. More importantly, we were anxious to provide an opportunity for those individuals who remember our past to put their memories on record. In this regard we were especially fortunate to have had the benefit of Douglas Rathbone's prodigious ability to recall what went on in the early years. It was only shortly after he helped us with this book that sadly he died unexpectedly.

The story of Greig Fester describes the progress and growth of one company in the large, but relatively little known, world of reinsurance. We are fortunate in having been able to grow against the background of an industry itself growing and changing rapidly. The fact that we have been successful in plotting a course through this ever-changing scene is a tribute to our predecessors whose vision, enthusiasm and high standards have been a constant inspiration.

Firstly, my thanks must go to Antony Brown, the author, whose zeal in researching and interpreting our world together with his highly readable style eminently qualified him to draw together the threads of the Greig Fester story. I would also like to thank Peter Keats, who has worked long and hard before and after his retirement to complete this project.

Finally, I very much hope that our readers – be they clients, staff, shareholders or the general public – will find this book to be of more than passing interest.

John S. Greig

Introduction

The last two decades have seen a notable increase in the range of non-technical books about insurance. Partly, no doubt, this is a consequence of the growing interest of ordinary readers in the international industry, but I believe another reason is the wider perception of how closely reinsurance in particular relates not only to world economic patterns but to the day-to-day dramas of world news. Yet until now remarkably little has been written, with the general reader in mind, on what is in so many ways the most fascinating and dramatic aspect of the whole craft.

It was against this background that John Greig suggested to me that a book about the firm founded by his father might tell not only the history of a remarkable company but would also reflect the story of modern reinsurance in which Greig Fester holds such a unique place. Insurance is about taking risks – and my first thanks must be to him for entrusting the writing of this story to someone so unversed in the skills and subtleties of the reinsurance scene. There followed many hours of patient explanation from John Greig himself and from Peter Keats, and they both have my best thanks. The late Douglas Rathbone was a mine of information on the reinsurance landmarks of Greigs' earlier days, and his friends and former colleagues will share my great regret that he did not live to see the publication of this book. I should also like to thank Brian Wallas for his hospitality and a wealth of anecdotes relating to Festers' earlier years.

All the Greig Fester staff mentioned in these pages have been most helpful in guiding me at all stages of the research, but I am particularly grateful to Dieter Losse for his illuminating perspective of reinsurance on the world scene. Desmond Graves helped to widen my horizons as to what happens when companies are merged, and I am specially indebted to Mrs Elspeth Shepherd, Walter Greig's daughter, for telling me about the family history and for her patience in answering numerous enquiries. Michael Berndt of Hamburg was a most valuable guide to the history of Mund & Fester. Jo Morgan and Janet Hill have been unfailingly patient and resourceful on the secretarial side, while David Macdonald was tireless in shepherding the book through the final stages of production. The team at Book Production Consultants plc have been most supportive and I must thank Stephanie Zarach in particular for her enthusiasm and tireless encouragement at all times.

I am most grateful to the Chairman and Directors of Lloyd's of London Press for permission to reprint a paragraph from D.E.W. Gibb's *Lloyd's of London: A Study in Individualism* and also for a quotation from an article by Mr Jim Bannister in *Lloyd's List*. My thanks are also due to *The Times* for permission to quote from a report on the 1954 Australian insurance losses, and to the Directors of Guardian Royal Exchange Assurance plc for allowing me to reprint two passages from Professor Barry Supple's *The Royal Exchange Assurance: A History of British Insurance 1720–1970*. Meanwhile no writer on reinsurance can fail to be indebted to C.E. Golding's 1927 history of reinsurance which remains, from the historical viewpoint, unchallenged as the standard work. This and other books consulted are noted on p 113.

Antony Brown

The background image on each chapter opening page shows a broker's slip from the period covered. The broker's slip is the form on which details of a particular risk or insured event requiring protection are entered. Each underwriter writes their name under these details along with the share of the risk accepted. This is the historical origin of the term 'underwriter'.

CHAPTER ONE

Early days

Avenida de Mayo, Buenos Aires, circa 1919

On New Year's Day in 1921, a passer-by in the City of London might have seen an engaging but slightly odd sight. Three energetic and excited-looking young men were getting out of a taxi which had just brought them from Charing Cross. As one of them paid the taxi, the second stacked a load of office files and papers on the pavement while the third reached down a coal scuttle which had been perched precariously on the taxi roof. New Year's Day had fallen on a Saturday that year, and in the 1920s Saturday until lunchtime was still a working day, and New Year's Day was not yet a holiday in England. Even so, there would probably have been few passing by to see the taxi with its unusual cargo as it progressed past St Paul's and Cannon Street before turning into Nicholas Lane, which still survives as part of the network of small courts and alleys threading through the City like a leaf's veins. The house where they stopped was No. 34, opposite the site of St Nicholas Church from which the lane took its name, quite a large block providing office-space for as many as fourteen firms.

No. 34 Nicholas Lane in the City of London, the site of the first office of W.T. Greig Ltd, and the surrounding area.

The young men getting out of the taxi with such enthusiasm were three brothers named Greig, and this New Year's Day was a landmark they had all been looking forward to for a long time. The middle brother, Walter, sparkling eyed and with a walk and bearing suggesting he was very much the leader, had until recently been a high-flyer at the Royal Exchange Assurance: it was now just two months since he had given in his notice in order to start his own firm. His brothers, Kenneth and Leonard, were to be his partners. The company was to

EARLY DAYS

be known as W.T. Greig Ltd, and its business was described as an insurance broker's.

It was a venture typical of its time, for in those restless post-war years many people were looking for a new start. True, there was much in the newspapers that New Year's Day to reflect the fact that, after the turmoil and tragedy of war, the country was settling down. At the Haymarket Theatre, Fay Compton was appearing in Sir James Barrie's *Mary Rose*, and the list of pantomimes was headed by Phyllis Dare at the Hippodrome in *Aladdin*. In Melbourne, the MCC team was beginning the second Test match of the Ashes tour. The New Year Honours List had brought a baronetcy for Baden-Powell, the founder of the Boy Scouts.

But the memories of war were still, almost nostalgically, strong. One advertiser in the personal column of *The Times* sent greetings to old comrades who might remember him from France. There were reports of a hilarious New Year's Eve party at a Victoria hotel, where the ecstatic revellers had been swooped on by an airship descending from the ceiling, and there had been a 'Bolshevik invasion' of the hotel's dining-room, followed by a 'battle of the Allies'. The saddest item in the paper was a news story about an ex-officer charged with street-begging as an organ-grinder. He had been remanded when someone from an old comrades' association had spoken for him.

The war had left its mark upon the Greigs too. Kenneth, the eldest, who was 37, had served throughout the war in France. Though Walter himself had been marooned through the war in Argentina, another brother, Roy, had been killed in March 1918. Leonard, the youngest brother, had been wounded and sent back to the front eight times.

But such memories would have been dispelled in the excitement of the moment as the brothers began organising the two rooms on the second floor which were to be the new firm's birthplace. Perhaps it may have seemed a good omen that Nicholas Lane, small as it was, already had a secure place in the history of insurance. It was only yards away, in the former Parsonage of St Nicholas, that in 1762 the Rector, the Revd Edward Mores, had been the first person to work out the mathematical principles of life assurance.

There was one other thing about the move to No. 34 Nicholas Lane, though it would have meant nothing to the brothers at the time. Until a few years previously – 1910, to be precise – one of the tenants renting space there had been a firm called Fester, Fothergill & Hartung. They had moved across Cannon Street by now, to new and larger premises in Laurence Pountney Lane, a still narrower and more winding example of the City's network of small streets.

Later their paths would cross again with Greigs, so that we might almost say that the January day in 1921 was the point at which the past and future of both companies started to become one.

Meanwhile, who were the Greigs, and what were the hopes and aspirations that had led them to set up their new firm?

Greigs, any Scot will tell you, were originally McGregors. The clan was proscribed in the early seventeenth century because of its unfortunate ways of sheep-stealing and reiving. Afterwards, the McGregors were forced either to emigrate or change their names, so we get such variants as Griggs, Greer, Grieg and Grieve. Most emigrating Greigs went to the USA or Canada, but a few went east: a Greig was Admiral of the Russian Fleet under Czar Nicholas, and Edvard Grieg, Norway's greatest composer, was a Scottish emigrant's great-grandson.

But the line with which this story is concerned begins with George Greig, a tallow chandler who in 1702 became a burgher of Kirkcaldy near Edinburgh. That is all we know about him – except that he married one of the two daughters of John Archer, who is described as a merchant from the small town of Leslie, twenty or so miles north of Kirkcaldy on the road to Perth.

Such bald facts might seem to make for a family biography that is conventional enough. But the Archer connection takes us into the realm of high drama straightaway, for both John Archer and his brother Thomas were Covenanters, or supporters of the Covenant of 1638 which had forced King Charles I to depose his bishops and to restore the Presbyterian system of the Scots. The result had been half a century of religious wars and bitter persecution for the faith. What form the persecution took for John Archer we do not know, but when we come to his brother Thomas, the facts are all too brutally clear. Captured after being wounded in a skirmish with the King's troops outside Edinburgh, he was hanged in the Grassmarket on 21 August 1685.

EARLY DAYS

'He was a worthy minister qualified to be a Professor of Divinity in any University,' his kinswoman Margaret Clunie proudly wrote on the flyleaf of his Bible which she bequeathed to her cousin, Betsy Greig, in 1828. 'I being near to my end wish to leave it to one who will be careful of it,' she added, and the Archer Bible has ever since been a treasured Greig possession.

Thomas Archer's example of courage and self-sacrifice would confer a sense of pride on any family, but the succeeding generations of Greigs were more concerned with the day-to-day business of raising a family and earning a living than with the violent extremes of faith which brought distress to so many Scottish homes in those years. George Greig's son David, born at Leslie, followed him into the candle-making trade, but the next generation finds the family moving from the workshop to the desk. David's son John, born five days before Christmas 1745, who seems to have steered the family back to Edinburgh when he became clerk to Scott, Smith and Stein, the bankers. Agnes Sibbald, his wife, was an Edinburgh girl, and two of their surviving sons, Thomas and John, went into the book trade. Thomas is recorded as setting up a printing partnership with John Walker in 1806 while John, two years his junior, was described as a bookseller and clerk to a firm called Manners and Miller.

This John Greig is the first recorded member of the family to be mentioned in connection with insurance. One of the few surviving family documents of the time is a policy which he took out with an insurance office whose name, tantalisingly, was Sievwright & Greig. The policy itself was for a

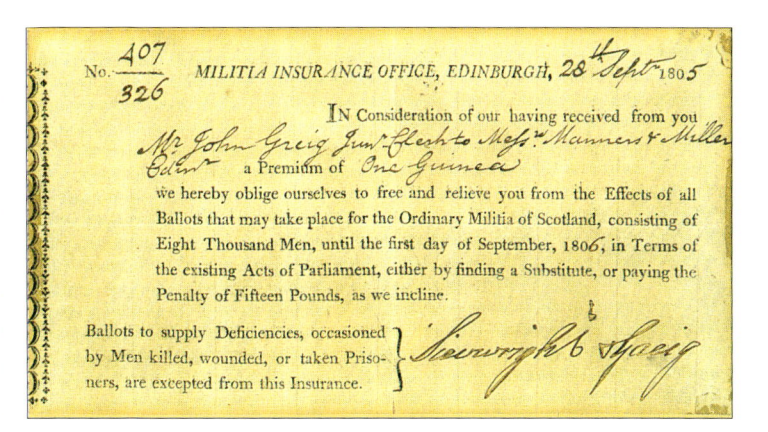

Militia insurance policies issued in 1805 and 1806 to John Greig. He was the first member of the family known to have a connection with insurance.

type of risk, not uncommon at the time, known as militia insurance. The point of it was that the Militia Act of 1802 had given county lord lieutenants the right to call up 8,000 men in Scotland to serve for five years. Anyone who was thus conscripted might avoid service either by being medically unfit or by finding a substitute who would serve instead of him for a £15 fee. If you had the bad luck to be called up but were insured, the insurer would find and pay a substitute for a premium of – in John Greig's case – one guinea. The policy was dated 28 September 1805, the year of Trafalgar, and was issued from the Militia Insurance Office, Edinburgh, and signed Sievwright & Greig.

Was John Greig, the insured, related to the Greig who was the insurer? It would seem not, for there is no record of his working for anyone except Manners and Miller, the booksellers. Moreover he lived to be only 38 and it seems hardly likely he would have moved from bookselling to the insurance business in such a short life.

Meanwhile with Thomas, his elder brother, we come to the first Greig who could be said to have steered the family fortunes onto a clear path. His printing business seems to have been mainly occupied with reprinting the classics – but evidently this was profitable, for he lived in some style. He bought a house in Buccleuch Place, an attractive square of bow-windowed houses in what is now Edinburgh's university quarter. Even today the houses there have a fine view of The Meadows park, and in his time they would have also looked towards the Holyroodhouse grounds. Before long Thomas was acquiring more property in the centre of Edinburgh – and must have seemed a confirmed bachelor when he was still unmarried at the age of 63. We have no record of what his relations thought when, in the first recorded mention of a Greig going south of the border, he married Rebecca Clunie, the daughter of a St Marylebone baker, at Paddington Church in London in 1847. John Andrew, their only child, was born two years later.

Thomas died at St Andrews in 1862, after which Rebecca seems to have come south again, for she died in 1878 in what the records call 'her son's house'. John Andrew would then have been 29: there are no records as to where he was educated, whether he worked in England or Scotland in his early years, or when he went south. Clearly he was still oriented to his Scottish birth, however, for in 1882 he married Annie Thomson, daughter of a wholesale stationer from Fern in Ross-shire.

EARLY DAYS

Four years later we find him in London, working in the West End branch of Sun Life Assurance.

John Andrew's story takes us from Edinburgh straight to the heartbeat of the capital, for the Sun Life's West End branch was in the street we know as Whitehall. In those days – in fact until 1931 – the section between Scotland Yard and Northumberland Avenue was still called Charing Cross, and the old street sign can still be seen there. The Sun Life building was at No. 60, between Blamey's the tailors and a shop called Matthews which sold, somewhat exotically, india rubber and mascara.

John Andrew began with a salary of £200 a year as resident secretary of the Charing Cross branch. His progress seems to have been steady but not spectacular: in 1905 he was promoted to district manager, with a salary of £850 which rose to £900 over two years. All the same it must have been a comfortable life with Annie and his five children – four boys and a girl (there had been another boy, Eric, who sadly died at the age of 7) – in their handsome house near Putney Heath, an almost rural spot in those days.

John Andrew Greig surrounded by his children (left to right) Walter, Lillias, Kenneth, Roy and Leonard, taken circa 1897 at Herne Bay.

The Sun Life Assurance's office in Charing Cross (now Whitehall) in 1912. **Above:** The general office with the Manager, John Andrew Greig, in the right foreground. **Right:** John Andrew Greig in his office.

EARLY DAYS

As to the office, the photographs taken in 1912 suggest a spacious Edwardian world where everything would proceed as it had always done, on smooth rails. It seems somehow suitable that John Andrew, born at the halfway mark of the nineteenth century, should have retired at the end of May 1914, two months before his comfortable world was to be changed for ever.

Meanwhile, the next generation of Greigs had already begun to follow their father into the insurance business. Kenneth and Leonard had started with his own firm, the Sun Life, and its parent, the Sun Fire, while Walter, then aged 20, had joined the Royal Exchange Assurance Corporation in 1904. Before we return to the three brothers in Nicholas Lane, we should look briefly at this famous insurance institution which, in shaping Walter's future, was to play a key part.

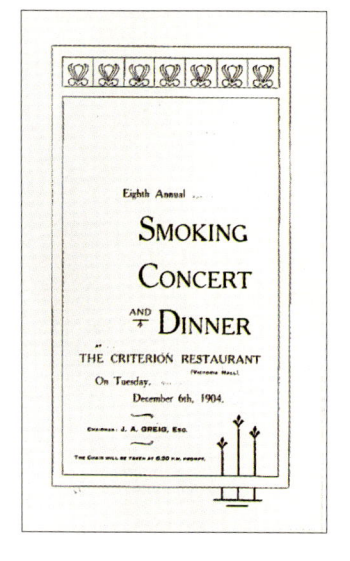

Programme of a concert and dinner at the Criterion Restaurant (Victoria Hall) chaired by John Andrew Greig in 1904.

The Royal Exchange Assurance Corporation has always been among the industry's great names. One of the very few companies whose history went back even further than the coffee-house set up by Edward Lloyd, its home had for almost two centuries been the historic building in the very heart of the City of London from which it took its name. Famous in a range of insurance classes from marine to fire, it had, nevertheless, during the later decades of the nineteenth century, become noted for a certain lack of adventurousness. This had begun to show especially in its neglect of overseas business in which its competitors were forcing the pace: in 1895, out of the Royal Exchange's total fire premiums of £143,000, only £3,000 came from abroad. This was compared to the Commercial Union's foreign premium of £600,000, and £360,000 for the Sun Fire office.

All this was to change dramatically in the years between 1886 and 1904 when Walter Greig joined. In 1891, the company had begun to underwrite in the USA, earning premiums of just on £17,000 in the first year. By the next year, *Post Magazine* was hailing the company's 'infusion of new blood', while rising foreign fire premiums began 'a new era in the Company's history and a new departure'.

The tendency towards overseas expansion was redoubled when Edward Hiles, who had been brought into the company as foreign clerk, was appointed one of two joint fire managers in 1902. Over the next eleven years the fire department almost doubled its overseas business, with foreign premiums soaring to £620,000. The Royal Exchange had become, says its historian Barry Supple, 'a worldwide fire office ... Barely 30 per cent of its premium income came from the United Kingdom.'

As always, this expansion was made possible by reinsurance which, later in this book, emerges as a major theme. For the moment we can define it simply as the way in which underwriters seek to offload part of their risk; by reinsuring they in effect insure themselves against the possibility of very large or unexpected claims. Through reinsurance, too, insurers can take on shares of risks in foreign markets whose social or political background they know little of. Reinsurance is not only the most intellectually interesting aspect of insurance but it is also very often the point at which the industry moves closest to the dramas and disasters which make world news.

With the Royal Exchange's expanding book of foreign business, reinsurance was bound to play a key role. There was, says Supple, 'a necessary and intricate skein of reinsurance arrangements through treaties and guarantees'. In the fire department, where Walter worked, most risks were ceded to the great continental companies and, in his later years, he would often deplore the time wasted on the infinitely tedious job of copying out, in longhand, the enormous lists of cessions that detailed the literally thousands of risks and the sum each was reinsured for. The process has been described by D.E.W. Gibb, the historian of Lloyd's:

> *The reinsurers ... all wanted to know just what risk they had been given. So the ceding company at regular intervals sent an elaborate bordereau to every company on its treaty and the reinsuring companies were supposed to note and enter all the lines in the bordereaux in their own books ... The truth may be ... that the system was continued only because man is a conservative animal, who will go on doing a lot of superfluous things for no better reason than that they always have been done.*

Douglas Rathbone, who worked with Walter Greig from 1928, commented: 'What he grasped, some years ahead of his time, was that no company would in any case be doing business with another unless there was trust between them. If you do trust them, then a simple statement once a quarter is enough.'

EARLY DAYS

Walter had worked at the Royal Exchange for eight years when there came the event that was to change his whole life. Over the previous twenty years the Corporation had been steadily building up its network of overseas branches. Among the oldest was the branch in Buenos Aires, and it was here that Walter was appointed branch manager in 1912. He was only 28, and the appointment clearly carried the promise of more promotion in the future.

Buenos Aires must have been an eye-opener for a young man fresh from Putney and the City offices of the Royal Exchange. The largest city of South America, it had, in 1912, all the springy excitement of a boom town – especially for its British community, who more than anyone had helped the Argentinians to tap their country's wealth. In 1873, it had been British engineers who had installed the city's drains and waterworks. The next decade had seen British investment in the nation's railways, while around the turn of the century Sir John Hawkshaw's massive scheme to build the city's docks had been implemented. All this had followed the efforts of the English, Irish and Scots farmers and miners who had braved the hazards of Argentina's hinterland to exploit its natural resources. Now, with a surging worldwide demand for Argentine beef, wheat, wool and hides, their trail-blazing was paying off handsomely. In 1912 the city itself sparkled with new buildings in the French Renaissance style, while squares planted with flowers and shrubs alternated with elaborately ornamented new business houses.

As for the English members of the exclusive Hurlingham Club, they seem almost to have lived the lives of eighteenth-century grandees. In his later years Walter Greig would recall how, as a young bachelor, he spent his days there: first came an hour's early-morning ride on his *rechazo*, or reject polo-pony. Then after showering he would proceed to breakfast, for which the Hurlingham Club's bachelor residents had a round table of their own. Then came the thirty-mile journey to the town's main railway station, the Retiro, named after the point to which the British Army had retreated in the 1808 battle for the city. From the station with its glass roof and splendid ironwork he would go to the Royal Exchange office in the Calle 25 de Mayo where he would open letters, do some dictation and then eventually stroll round to the

Illuminated address of thanks presented to Walter Greig by his associates at Leng Roberts on his departure from Buenos Aires in 1919.

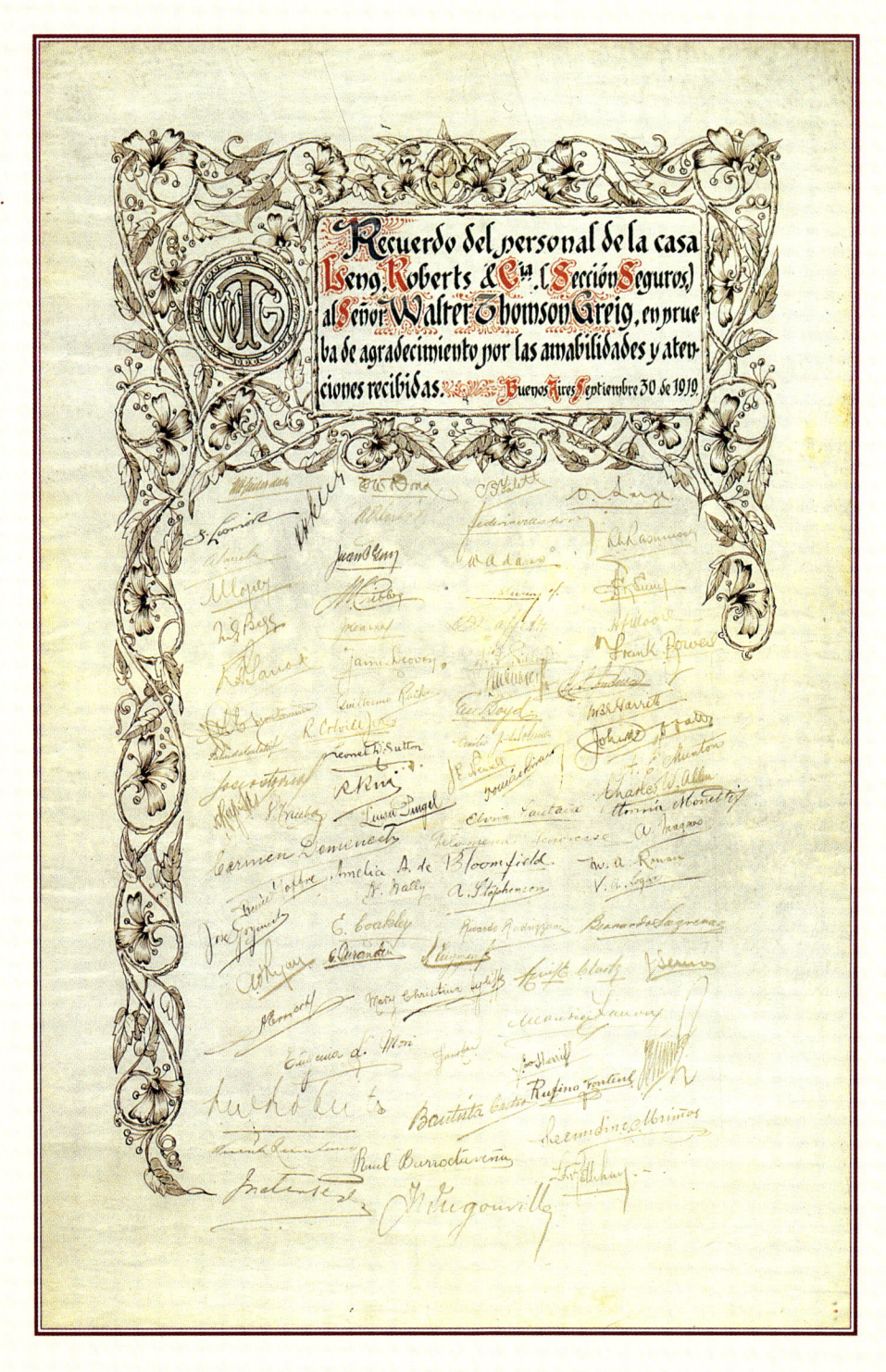

Early days

Extranjeros Club for lunch, after which there would be letters to sign, and perhaps people to see. The day's work seldom amounted to more than four hours.

Back at the Hurlingham Club there would be more sport, with a choice ranging from polo to football. Cricket and golf had flourished in Argentina since 1872, despite the heavy import duty payable on golf clubs. In order to counter this duty, the ingenious British (it was said) used to stroll down to Sir John Hawkshaw's new docks, then come back with the clubs which they used as walking sticks to outwit the customs officials.

There was a more serious aspect to Walter Greig than the Hurlingham Club's lifestyle might suggest. All through his life one has the impression of a thoughtful, highly receptive mind that was for ever seeking opportunities and making plans. One consequence of his being suddenly thrown in at the deep end in the Buenos Aires office was a lifelong enthusiasm for languages: knowing no Spanish before, he took intensive lessons on the Royal Mail boat out. In later years, when he spoke fluent Spanish and good German, he would tell his daughter Elspeth how much he regretted that he had not learnt to speak fluent French at the school where he and his brothers had been at Putney. As to business, though it proceeded at a gentler pace than nowadays, he rapidly made himself a major figure on the Buenos Aires scene. Among the friendships he formed, there was one, with R.W. – known always as Bobbie – Roberts of the Anglo–Argentine finance house, Leng Roberts, that was to bear much fruit in the future. Through Bobbie Roberts he would, for example, develop close links with Baring Brothers.

Meanwhile his letters back to the London head office are full of a quiet confidence about handling business matters. 'I am indeed fortunate in the opportunity of doing my best guided by methods and intentions I know I can trust ... the Chile question is at rest and that of new offices also for the present', he writes to Ferrers Daniell, who had been appointed joint fire manager with Edward Hiles in the year that Walter had set out.

At the same time he seems to have taken a realistic view of the possibilities of business.

I should think that this country will go ahead soon, especially as crop prospects are very bright indeed. When the improvement starts I hope to wake things up [in] the country, which business I have deliberately allowed to go slack this year. It has not been worth doing, poor risks, financially in difficulties and probably bad debts instead of the premiums.

The correspondence takes on a more sombre tone with the outbreak of war, as we see from his letter to Daniell on 19 August 1914:

I wrote you a private letter last week and sent a duplicate. I am afraid, however, that the duplicate went on the same boat and as I would like you to receive it I am sending a copy herewith. We get very little news from England and as yet the Consul has no news of what will happen to the volunteers who left for England this week.

The Greig brothers (left to right), Walter, Kenneth and Leonard, in the uniform of the London Scottish territorial regiment.

All Walter's letters at this time are concerned with the possibilities of volunteering – and there is a note of dismay at being so far from home, especially when he and his brothers, who were already in France, had been enthusiastic part-time soldiers with the London Scottish. 'I wish to volunteer, if men are required, and am ambitious to do my duty. If I thought it my duty not to volunteer, then if an appeal were made for them I should find it very difficult to face public opinion here, the more so being, by my position, among the more prominent young Englishmen,' he wrote later the same month.

He was also, understandably, feeling that home was very far off. 'We certainly live in extraordinary times, and had I known of them when you called me into your room in February 1912 and asked me if I would go to the Argentine, I think I should have endeavoured, at least to stipulate for leave in July 1914,' he writes to Daniell on 5 November. In another letter he again brings up the subject of volunteering: 'I am not grumbling at staying here so long as it is right, but what I do claim is to be the first of the people in similar positions to me to go ... I dread coming short of what is right.'

The head-office view, apparently, was that he should not volunteer, for in November he feels he 'must either wait a cable from London or have sufficient grounds to appeal against your decision'. What added to his previous intention of joining up was the news, mentioned elsewhere in the letter, that 'it is true that the London Scottish are in the firing line. This makes me very restless.'

A week later, however, he is writing to Daniell with good news from the front:

> *I have a cable from my Father today saying that my three brothers with the London Scottish are safe which I expect does not mean that they are in a safe place but that they are well ... It is difficult to know when this war will end, the most optimistic opinion which I consider sound is the end of March.*

Walter formally volunteered that November, only to be told that he was of more use in his Buenos Aires job. Three months later he became ill with appendicitis, complicated by a hernia, which effectively ruled him out of military service. The whole question seems to have ended with a letter from the Military Attaché of the British Legation in Buenos Aires in August 1918, stating:

> *I beg leave to inform you that the Commission having carefully considered your position, has decided that you should not offer yourself for Military Service. An Exemption Certificate signed by the Minister and the Military Attaché will be issued to you in due course.*

Fourteen months later he was back in London. On 13 November he received a letter from Percy Hodge, Secretary of the Royal Exchange (a position which roughly corresponded to what nowadays we should call chief executive), promoting him to the post of Assistant Fire Manager.

Beneath the signature at the bottom of the letter are Walter's draft notes for his reply. 'I trust I shall merit the confidence that the Directors have thus placed in me,' he wrote – then 'I trust I shall' is crossed out. 'I shall do my utmost to' is what he wrote instead, and you can almost hear his tone of resolution.

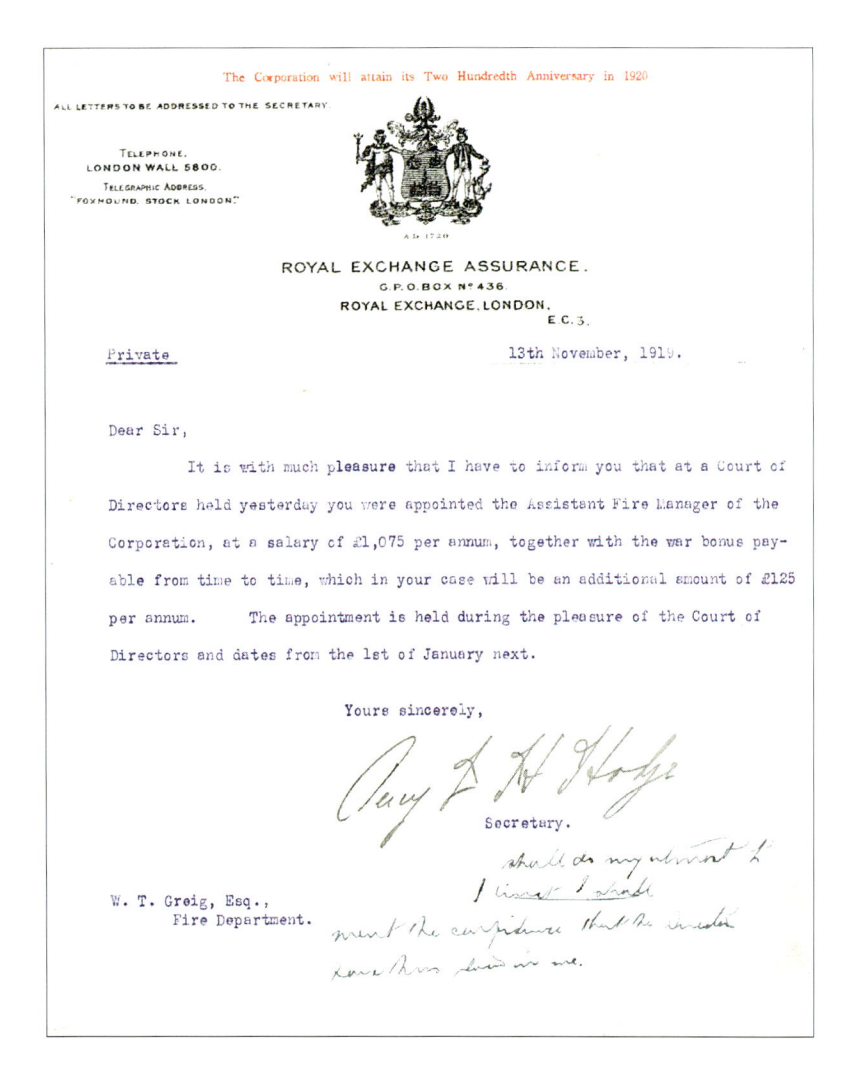

> ROYAL EXCHANGE ASSURANCE.
> G.P.O. BOX Nº 436
> ROYAL EXCHANGE, LONDON.
> E.C.3.
>
> Private   13th November, 1919.
>
> Dear Sir,
>
> It is with much pleasure that I have to inform you that at a Court of Directors held yesterday you were appointed the Assistant Fire Manager of the Corporation, at a salary of £1,075 per annum, together with the war bonus payable from time to time, which in your case will be an additional amount of £125 per annum. The appointment is held during the pleasure of the Court of Directors and dates from the 1st of January next.
>
> Yours sincerely,
>
> [signature] Secretary.
>
> W. T. Greig, Esq.,
>   Fire Department.

It was in those days an amazing promotion for a young man of thirty-five. Over him, in one of the world's largest insurance companies, there would be only the Secretary himself and three departmental heads. Clearly the directors meant to make the best use of his talents, for soon he was using his languages again: this time on a trip to see the company's branch office and agencies in Cuba, where there were problems over claims for sugar-crop insurance.

The Royal Exchange were clearly delighted with their new young Assistant Fire Manager. Yet a year later Mr Hodge was writing once more:

EARLY DAYS

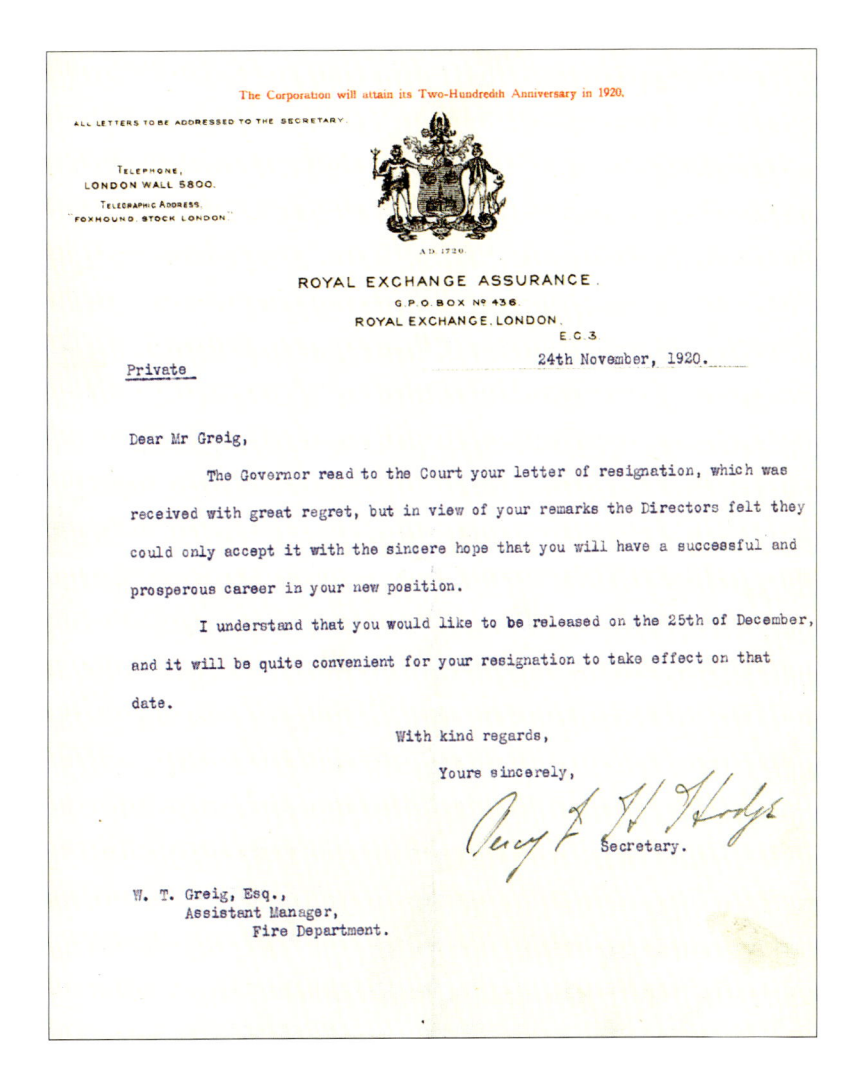

> The Corporation will attain its Two-Hundredth Anniversary in 1920.
>
> ALL LETTERS TO BE ADDRESSED TO THE SECRETARY.
>
> TELEPHONE,
> LONDON WALL 5800.
>
> TELEGRAPHIC ADDRESS,
> "FOXHOUND, STOCK, LONDON."
>
> **ROYAL EXCHANGE ASSURANCE.**
> G.P.O. BOX No. 436.
> ROYAL EXCHANGE, LONDON.
> E.C.3.
>
> 24th November, 1920.
>
> Private
>
> Dear Mr Greig,
>
> The Governor read to the Court your letter of resignation, which was received with great regret, but in view of your remarks the Directors felt they could only accept it with the sincere hope that you will have a successful and prosperous career in your new position.
>
> I understand that you would like to be released on the 25th of December, and it will be quite convenient for your resignation to take effect on that date.
>
> With kind regards,
>
> Yours sincerely,
>
> Percy F. N. Hodge
> Secretary.
>
> W. T. Greig, Esq.,
>   Assistant Manager,
>   Fire Department.

Why, within a year of receiving as glittering a promotion as any young man could wish, did Walter decide to set up his own firm? Partly the idea must have been in his mind before he ever left Buenos Aires – the key to it being his close relationship with Bobbie Roberts, whose own firm, Leng Roberts, controlled two of Argentina's largest insurance companies, La Buenos Aires and La Rosario. And what seems certain is that he promised Walter that he should have their reinsurances to offer on the London market if he ever decided to set up his own firm.

Was there another reason too? The fortunes of the rest of the family were not as glittering as Walter's own. Despite his efforts to join up, he had spent the last years agreeably enough in Argentina, but the other Greigs had suffered grievously, with one brother, Roy, killed in the last months of the war. Leonard Greig was still in constant pain from the headaches that were the legacy of four years at the front. Now both he and Kenneth had come home to humdrum jobs with no great promise of more interesting things to come.

To Walter, travelled, successful, highly paid, it was all a sharp contrast to his own life. What he was really seeking to achieve, it must have seemed, as the brothers unloaded their taxi in Nicholas Lane on New Year's Day, was an enterprise in which they could all share.

CHAPTER TWO

Festers and the European scene

The city of Antwerp, where Mund & Fester was founded in 1874

When Walter Greig set up his business with his brothers in 1921, he was quite sure of one thing: he was going to specialise in reinsurance. Doubtless this was partly because of his experience with the Royal Exchange. There was also the promise of business from his Buenos Aires friend, Bobbie Roberts.

To many people in 1921, however, it might have seemed an odd choice. For in London, reinsurance was still regarded as something of a sideline, a tributary of the mainstream of insurance business. It was a very different scene on the Continent where reinsurance had been in use from the earliest times for marine risks. On a voyage from Genoa to Sluys as far back as 1371 there was a record of an underwriter reinsuring the most hazardous part – from Cadiz to Sluys – while retaining his own liability for the Genoa–Cadiz stretch in the western Mediterranean's relatively safe seas.

But marine reinsurance was forbidden in England under an Act of 1746 which made it unlawful to reinsure unless the original insurer died or became insolvent. Why the traditionally inventive London market missed out on reinsurance is not clear. One reason may be that most of London's more innovative ideas had always come from Lloyd's – and by its nature Lloyd's underwriting method was based on the sharing of a risk. Whatever the reason, there seems no doubt that, by the turn of the eighteenth century, London lagged behind the rest of the Continent. C.E. Golding, Britain's most eminent historian of reinsurance, quotes a Lincoln's Inn lawyer, James Park, who noted in 1800 that marine reinsurance had 'obtained a place in most of the commercial systems of the trading powers of Europe and is allowed by them to be politic and legal'.

Nevertheless, the earliest recorded treaty was not on the Continent but in the USA. It came when the Eagle Fire Company of New York agreed in August 1813 to reinsure all the outstanding fire risks of the Union Insurance Company for a premium of $2,590.83. Europe's first known agreement seems to have been that between the Compagnie

Royale of Paris and the Compagnie des Propriétaires Réunis of Brussels, dated 15 December 1821 – a century, almost to the day, before Walter Greig set up his own firm.

Thirty years or so later came the beginnings of the great German reinsurance firms, starting with the Cologne Re in 1853 and leading to the establishment of the mighty Munich Re in 1880.

London's record over the same period was in meagre contrast. Between 1867 and 1877 there were four reinsurance companies in the City, none of which survived more than a few years. All the same, there were frequent deals between the companies. The Sun, for instance, exchanged premiums with the Phoenix between 1844 and 1867, receiving premiums of £24,130 and paying losses of £17,666. The reciprocal business seems to have worked slightly in favour of the Sun: over the same period, the Phoenix accepted premiums of £19,263 from the Sun and paid losses and expenses of £25,626. Later the Phoenix was to take something of a lead among British companies as a reinsurer: in 1862, notes its historian Clive Trebilcock, it placed a large treaty with the Storebrand Insurance Company of Norway, where fire premiums had climbed after Christiania, the capital, was ravaged by fire in 1858. Another notable Phoenix deal was a £6,000 reinsurance of a hazardous cotton mill in Calcutta which it placed with the West of Scotland Company, noted as an active reinsurer.

The Mercantile & General, set up in 1907, was Britain's first important company devoted purely to reinsurance: it was followed in the immediate pre-war years by twelve others, few of which survived long. Indeed, it is a measure of London's lack of interest in the concept as a whole that on 5 August 1914, the fire managers of all the leading companies were thrown into a state of panic – not so much fearing the disasters of war as realising that, for the foreseeable future, the foreign (especially the German) companies were not going to be around to reinsure them. In the end the fire managers are said to have been so anxious to find homes for their reinsurances that they spent the first day of war on the telephone, asking each other to take a proportion of their treaties.

It could be said to have been the day when the London market first ventured into reciprocal reinsurance. Its effect wore off considerably when, in November 1918, they all went back to their traditional continental reinsurers – though the next year was to see a new upsurge of ten companies, including the Victory and the Treaty Re.

Meanwhile there is one significant figure we have not mentioned yet: the reinsurance broker.

The reinsurance broker had, perhaps surprisingly, been around for some while. As far back as 1829 there are records of a broker named Cazenove in Broad Street offering a fire treaty from the Union of Paris to the Royal Exchange – a project which, it seems, was turned down. The next name after Cazenove is that of Martin Heckscher, who set up in St Petersburg in 1865 as a reinsurance broker and agent for several London companies including the Imperial Fire Office and the Commercial Union.

The mention of St Petersburg – that graceful city which Peter the Great built to convince himself and his fellow-countrymen that they were truly Europeans – seems somehow to take us to the very heart of nineteenth-century reinsurance. For reinsurance had grown up in the northern European world: if there is a pattern to be discerned in its development, it is that it grew most vigorously in those lands on the Baltic and the North Sea ports which had produced the Hanseatic merchants – who in their turn had been the forefathers of insurance. It was a vastly different world from that of the Greig brothers with their taxi-load of files and a coal scuttle. Yet in a remarkable way the two traditions would become one.

For among these shadowy figures with their invariably foreign names there is one who very much concerns us. His name was Carl Hartung and, for some time prior to 1874, he had been manager of the Imperial Fire Office. In that year he had resigned in order to set up a London agency for a Russian insurance company called the Jakor Insurance Company. Five years later Carl Hartung died, but not before he had taken his brother Frederick into the firm in what seems to have been a partnership. Where Frederick had been prior to this we do not know.

But their name draws us closer to the subject of this book. For Fester, Fothergill & Hartung was, you may remember, the firm which had preceded the Greig brothers into Nicholas Lane.

Top: Heinrich Fester, who with Adolph Mund founded Mund & Fester in Antwerp in 1874. Two years later, his brother Jules (**below**) set up the Hamburg branch of the company.

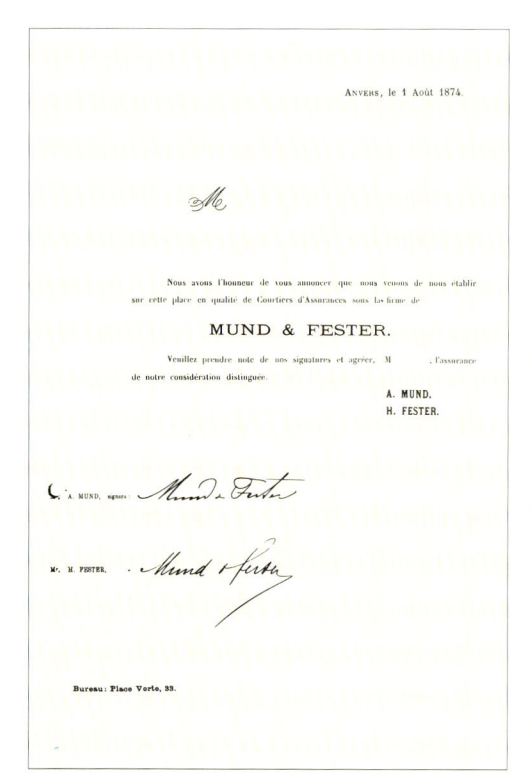

Announcement of the establishment of Mund & Fester in 1874.

The Hartung brothers' firm was still not a broking house in the way we understand the term today. Its original role as an agency would have been to write business on behalf of the Jakor. But, as today, the business would have been in a true sense international, and Frederick Hartung must have travelled widely. One of his ports of call would have been St Petersburg – by now, even apart from the Jakor connection, an important reinsurance centre – where he would have visited Martin Heckscher.

He would also certainly have been to Antwerp, which had been famous as a European insurance centre long before the days of Lloyd's coffee-house. Here, in 1874 – the same year that Carl Hartung had set up the Jakor agency in London – an Antwerp broker named Heinrich Fester had begun a reinsurance broking business at Place Verte 33. Like so much in the reinsurance business, the firm could hardly have been more cosmopolitan, for Heinrich was a German whose family had come from Frankfurt. His partner in the Antwerp firm was another German named Adolph Mund and, in 1876, Mund & Fester opened a Hamburg office, run by Heinrich's brother, Jules.

The point at which Frederick first made contact with Mund & Fester is not recorded, but an atmosphere of trust obviously developed, for in 1896 they set up a London branch, taking Frederick into partnership. The firm was then named Mund, Fester & Hartung. It was part of an international expansion that must have seemed remarkable in those days, but Heinrich Fester seems to have been possessed of an almost Rothschild-like panache, for between 1900 and 1910 he sent all his sons to work in branches of the family firm that by then existed in Copenhagen, St Petersburg, Antwerp, Hamburg and London.

But now another strand was interwoven. It would bring, to English ears at least, a somewhat homelier place-name to the story of the Festers, Munds and Hartungs.

Festers and the European scene

Liverpool had been a notable name in insurance since the beginning of the nineteenth century, when the Liverpool Underwriters Association had run its business almost like a local Lloyd's, with its sixteen private underwriting firms who sat in the Old Exchange Rooms. 'They were handsome and spacious, and fitted with a row of boxes similar to those now in use by the members of Lloyd's', noted one of the original subscribers. 'It was usual for the Secretary, on the occurrence of an important casualty, to mount a pedestal and announce such information to the subscribers.'

The underwriting power of the sixteen must have been considerable, for some of the leading firms accepted lines of up to £100,000 on an individual risk for their own names. But as the century went on,

Lloyd's Subscription Rooms in 1800. A coloured lithograph from a print by J. C. Stadler after Pugin and Rowlandson.

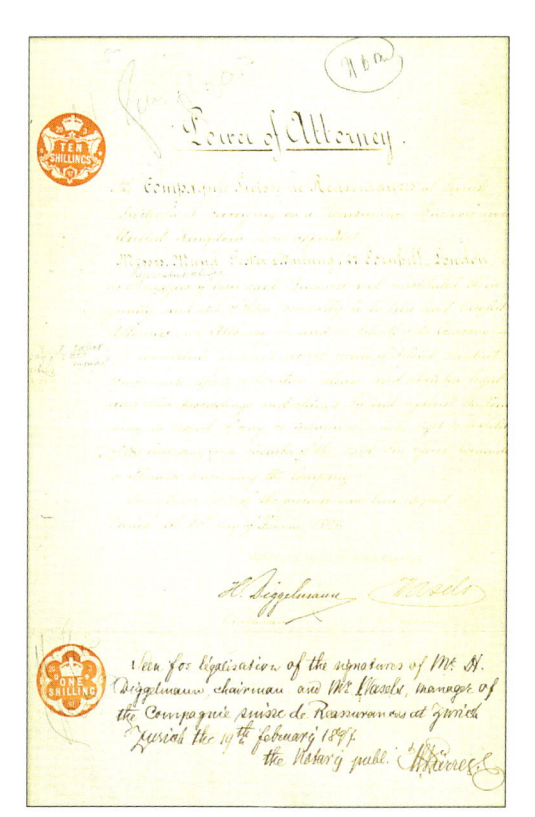

Certificate conferring power of attorney upon Mund, Fester & Hartung of London on behalf of the Compagnie Suisse de Réassurances, Zurich (the Swiss Re) in 1897.

companies began to replace the Liverpool private underwriters. Among the first was the Union Marine, set up in 1863, followed by the Standard Marine nine years later. Most notable among the non-marine companies was the Royal, dating from 1845.

The most significant from the point of view of Mund & Fester, though, was the London & Lancashire Fire, set up in 1861. The company's main guiding spirit in its early years was Henry Fothergill who, in 1871, had appointed Adolph Mund as his company's representative in Antwerp, and no doubt it was a consequence of the amiable atmosphere between the two companies that when, in 1897, Mund & Fester decided to start a branch in Liverpool, the person they chose as a local partner was Basil Fothergill, the son of their good friend in the London & Lancashire. Twelve years later Mund & Fester's two British branches merged, and there was born the London reinsurance broker Fester, Fothergill & Hartung.

We shall return to the story of the new company that thus appeared on the London scene for the first time; for the moment, though, it is perhaps enough to note the extreme contrast between the two groups whose paths would eventually converge. The one, as we have seen, had not much more to back it than the brimming energy, intelligence and confidence of a young man setting up his own business because he believed in it. The other, steeped in international tradition, was the product of a century's experience of Europe's most deeply sophisticated market. The possible combination was an intriguing and tantalising one. But for many years yet, the two would follow their own paths.

The introduction to this book suggested that one of its main themes would be to report on Greig Fester's contribution to international reinsurance. That might in turn suggest two kinds of reader: professional insurance people on the one hand and, on the other, the increasing number of non-technical people who find themselves intrigued by the London insurance market and its place on the world scene. With the latter group in mind, it may be helpful to add a word or two on how reinsurance actually works. Professionals, therefore, should now move on to Chapter 3. For the rest of us, what follows is intended as a simple guide.

REINSURANCE

Reinsurance can be described in a number of ways. Journalists like to compare it with the way that bookies hedge their bets; the Oxford Dictionary, in more stately style, describes it as an insurance 'by which an insurer or underwriter secures himself wholly or in part against the risk he has undertaken'.

More pictorially, one might also visualise it as being rather like the construction of an Elizabethan house, where a complicated set of vertical and horizontal beams, posts and struts are linked and interwoven in order to support a roof that is guaranteed to keep out storms and blizzards. And storms and blizzards, literally as well as metaphorically, beset anyone who sets up as an insurer. We take out insurance so that we can sleep at nights. But who takes care of the insurer's sleep?

Let us think of our insurer in cartoon terms – referring, for clarity, to 'him', despite the increasingly important role of women in insurance markets. The first thing an insurer must do, once he has begun writing policies, is to spread his risks. Unless he does this, he cannot afford to take on more risks.

Suppose he has begun his company with capital of £50 million. He hopes to attract a great many clients who will insure with him and this means he must write as much business as he can get. But if he is going to depend entirely on his own resources, and if all the properties he insures catch fire, his £50 million may not cover all his losses. Therefore, to write as much business as possible, he must increase his margin of safety beyond his basic capital.

So he takes out reinsurance – which is in essence a substitute for capital. In order to maximise his profits and still make sure he has the best possible protection, he must decide how much he can afford to lose on each risk he insures. This means striking a delicate balance between how much he retains – keeps for himself – and how much he cedes, or gives to the reinsurer.

There are three time-honoured forms of reinsurance. The first, known as facultative, means that the insurer looks at an individual risk, decides how much he wants to retain and then offers the balance to the reinsurer who has the right to decline or accept it.

But, assuming that the insurer has by now sold thousands of policies, it is going to be a time-consuming task to handle every single individual risk in this way. So he does a deal with his reinsurer – or reinsurers, for he may need the resources of several of them. What he arranges with them is a proportional treaty, under which he is bound to cede, and the reinsurers are bound to accept, a certain proportion of each risk. These cessions are made on a wholesale basis without the reinsurers having to be informed of the individual details of each risk.

This proportional treaty can take two forms. The first, the quota share treaty, consists simply of a fixed percentage of each risk being ceded to the reinsurers.

But the snag about this is that the insurer is then committed to ceding the same percentage of the small risks as of the large – whereas he might have been able to retain a much larger share of the small risks. Also some risks will be much more hazardous than others: suppose our insurer's portfolio includes a great many private houses and an industrial estate. And suppose also that at one end of the industrial estate is a small factory turning out designer clothes. It is well managed by a safety-conscious ownership, and there is no fire risk. But at the other end of the estate there is one of the insurer's classic hazards – a sawmill, vulnerable because a thrown-away cigarette could cause a fire.

The quota share system is not going to help our insurer to meet these conflicting needs because it is not going to differentiate between them. Instead, our insurer will ask his reinsurers to grant him what is called a surplus treaty. Under this he can vary the amount he retains or cedes by building up what are known as lines – a line being the amount the insurer retains on each reinsured risk. Thus a ten-line treaty means that for each line he retains the insurer can accept another ten, the key point being that the amount he can cede is always related to his retention. In this way, the reinsurer and the cedants are said to follow each other's fortunes. For example, on the designer

Festers and the european scene

A scene typical of the devastation caused across southern England by the hurricane of October 1987.

clothes factory, our insurer might decide he wants to keep half. So if it is insured for £2 million he will retain £1 million. But when it comes to the sawmill, he will not want to risk more than £100,000 of his own capital. The reinsurers will make up the rest – but only to the multiple of ten of the insurer's own stake.

By now we have seen our insurer gradually building up his reinsurance protection using a variety of means, securing his book of business as the Elizabethan roof is secured by its endless criss-cross of sturdy beams. But even now there is another potentially threatening area of risk. We saw the insurer thinking of the sawmill as a worse risk than the clothing factory or a private house – but what about a situation where he could be ruined if there was severe damage to a great many of the private houses all at once? Lightning does, after all, strike at many places at the same time, as the whole of southern England learnt in the hurricane of October 1987. The insurance business describes such an event as a catastrophe, and the 1987 hurricane was technically known in the business as CAT87J – CAT for catastrophe, 87 for the year, and J, the tenth letter of the alphabet, because it was the tenth catastrophe since the beginning of the year.

How does reinsurance cater for such wholesale disasters? Because their business is so much concerned with them, insurers and reinsurers have a special phrase: they speak of an insurance covering any one event. This might be an earthquake destroying the homes and businesses of hundreds of policyholders, a plane crash causing the pay-out of billions of dollars in liability claims or a North Sea storm bringing about the destruction of several oil-rigs.

To protect himself against such possibilities the insurer takes out the form of reinsurance called excess of loss. This is designed to protect him from having to pay out for disasters on the grand scale. Typically, it might guarantee to pay him £1.5 million on every loss arising out of any one event in excess of £500,000. In other words the original insurer would pay his basic £500,000 while the reinsurer pays everything above that. Excess of loss, as we shall see later on, is the most dramatic and demanding of all forms of modern reinsurance, and one in which Greig Fester specialises.

Meanwhile, our anxious insurer may feel that even now he does not have adequate cover for all his risks. If so he can go on from here: he can buy a second, even a third excess of loss policy, and indeed there is nothing to stop him going on reinsuring to the point where all the premium he has earned from his clients is used up in buying reinsurance. But before he reaches that point he will also have seen that knowing how much to retain and how much to reinsure is the insurer's true skill. This was the intriguing area in which, in January 1921, Walter Greig began laying the foundations of his business.

CHAPTER THREE

Honeymoon

A street scene in Havana in the early 1920s, the first business stop made by Walter and Mildred Greig on their honeymoon voyage

The story of the early years of the company is very much the story of the brilliance and magnetism that shone through everything Walter Greig did, and the fortunes of the new firm were to soar dramatically following a combination of happy circumstances that linked both to Walter's honeymoon and the good offices of the London Scottish sergeant-cook. But before that triumphant wedding march there would be, following the brothers' arrival at Nicholas Lane, an opening movement in a somewhat lower key. Said Douglas Rathbone, who joined the brothers in 1928:

In those early days there must have been weeks on end when they had very little to do. If there were no new contracts or modifications to organise, then the day-to-day routine of accounting procedures was all that happened in the office. Even in my time WT spent a lot of the day reading The Times. *Occasionally he would put on his morning coat and top hat to go and see one of the companies, but only if there was something to be done, which wasn't very often.*

As late as the end of the 1930s, Douglas Rathbone estimated, he could have made a note of all the firm's important transactions on the back of a postcard – though one reason for this was that the business consisted of several large contracts rather than many small ones. This was in the nature of the reciprocal reinsurance business in which Greigs specialised, and to which we must briefly now turn.

Reciprocal reinsurance has been defined as an extension of the idea of the spread of risk, which is the fundamental principle of all insurance. It is based on the idea that an insurance company could save itself cash if, instead of going to a professional reinsurer, it merely did a deal to swap risks with another direct insurer. Such an exchange would usually be between companies in different parts of the world, so there would be no danger of both companies facing a great many claims of the same type at the same time. Both sides would pay each other a premium in the normal way – though each would be hoping for an incoming flow of profits more or less the same as was paid out.

Walter Greig had a number of things going for him when he set up his insurance broking business in this field. First, the London companies had mostly only ever traded reciprocal treaties with their European friends – and with each other, as we saw, in 1914. The Argentine companies whose agencies he held were not only in a new part of the world from the London offices' point of view but they could also show a good management record and a good loss ratio. When he offered the British companies some profitable business from La Buenos Aires and La Rosario, they were happy to give the Argentine companies a significant share of their own risks.

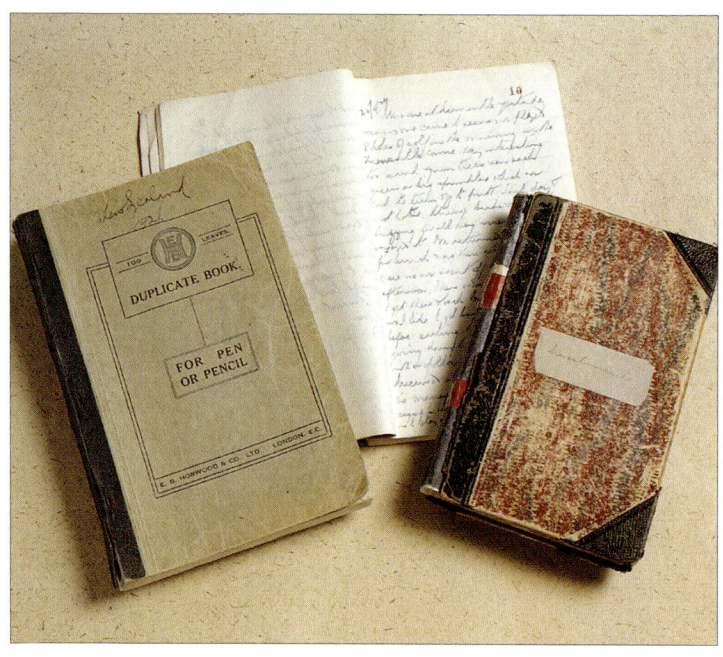

Walter Greig's original travel notebooks, preserved in the Greig Fester archives.

The second point in Walter's favour was that the concept of a broker dealing principally in reciprocal treaties was unusual for the London market. Of the large Lloyd's broking houses, relatively few would handle reinsurance and most of those would be capable of handling only facultative business. Sterling Offices and Festers, certainly with Russia prior to 1917, would have been among the rare exceptions to this rule.

Thirdly, insurance brokers deal in personalities as well as policies. With his charm, self-confidence and style, Walter Greig was entering a business for which he was eminently suited.

Even so, profits were somewhat modest in the brothers' first years. Much the most important income between 1921 and 1925 came from commission on the London companies' treaties with La Buenos Aires and La Rosario: by 1925, the year's commission from Argentina and London was £4,099. More modest earnings came from La Metropolitana of Cuba, with whom Walter, in 1922, had set up a fire treaty on his first trip abroad for his own firm. More important for the future would be the fire treaty exchange he had arranged between La Rosario and the Queensland of Australia while, apart from these reciprocal deals, the firm had also a small direct insurance section. This was presided over by Leonard Greig, and in 1924 it produced nearly a fifth of the total income of around £5,000. Modest as this seems today, it was not an inadequate living for the three brothers – whose main outgoings were their rent and a secretary – at a time when the tea-leaves' traditional forecast of '£1,000 a year and a handsome wife' was what most people would aspire to. In fact the deal originally set up between the brothers provided for the profits being divided equally, in thirds up to the first £3,000. Thereafter, Walter would get three-fifths and each of his brothers a remaining one-fifth.

Arguably, too, it was a time when people were less acquisitive and more content. For Leonard Greig, often sitting in the office clutching his head in pain, it must have been enough that he was no longer on the Western Front listening to the crash of shellfire. The motorcar and the telephone had arrived, but were not yet the tyrants over city and office life that they would soon be. Few people besides Walter Greig and the bank messengers wore the traditional top hat and tails, yet the City was still a place of almost Victorian ways where even close associates and friends would call each other not by first names but by initials.

In 1925, two events were to change things greatly for the Greigs. One was the result of an unusual business contact. The other event concerned Walter in particular. He had got his thousand a year. Now he was about to get a handsome wife.

Mildred Rowe joined the company in 1925 as Walter Greig's secretary. Romance flowered and they were married on 8 February 1926.

The first of the two events which were to open up new horizons for both Walter and his business came in 1925 when Mildred Rowe began work as his secretary. Brown haired and blue eyed, she was then 22, which made her nineteen years his junior.

Not noticeably pretty but highly intelligent and drily humorous, she came from Weymouth in Dorset where her grandfather, Thomas Rowe, had run the Royal Hotel. Other Rowes had carved successful careers in a variety of professions: Mildred's own father ran the local haulage firm, while one uncle was editor of the *Dorset Daily Echo*, and another – a good talking-point for Walter with his Latin American connections – was the manager of a flour mill in Rio de Janeiro.

Honeymoon

How long the romance between them took to flower we do not know, though Leonard Greig is said to have been shocked to find her sitting on his brother's desk, so Mildred seems unlikely to have been over-bashful. It has been said that a good wife takes on her husband's age and, between her intelligence and maturity and Walter's youthful energy and dash, the age-gap would rapidly have dwindled. In later years, their daughter Elspeth remembers, there seemed to be no age difference between them. They were married on 8 February 1926 and eleven days later left Liverpool on a honeymoon voyage to Australia and New Zealand which must have seemed to a 23-year-old girl in those days the height of romance.

The other aspect of the honeymoon is that it had a business side which, in its way, was almost as beguiling. Sometime during the winter of 1925–6, Walter had met a man named George Ritchie who was Chairman of the National Insurance Company of New Zealand. Their meeting had come about through someone close to the Greig brothers' hearts: before the war, all three had served as territorials in the London Scottish – the regiment with which Leonard and Kenneth had gone to France in the first weeks of the war. Among their London Scottish friends had been James Galbraith, who had been a notable figure in the regiment because he had the important job of sergeant-cook.

Professionally, James Galbraith had in those days been a clerk in the London office of a New Zealand company named the National Mortgage and Agency Company which, among other things, acted as a marine insurance-claims settling agency for the National Insurance Company's clients in London. After the war he had been promoted to manager of the London office and, because of the working link with the National Insurance Company, he found that one of his functions was to entertain that company's Chairman on his London visits. Sometime around the beginning of 1926, Galbraith had arranged a meeting between Ritchie and his old friends, the Greigs.

At this meeting Walter told Ritchie about the developing importance of reciprocal reinsurance. For the New Zealander, the concept was entirely new, but he was intrigued by it and told Walter that his company would like to learn more. It was almost precisely the moment at which Walter was planning his honeymoon and, as his son John observes, 'who could resist a tax-deductible honeymoon for six months?'

There was, however, one potential snag on the business side. George Ritchie explained to Walter that the company's General Manager, Mr Mallard, had somewhat old-fashioned views and would almost certainly be resistant to any such new-fangled scheme as reciprocal reinsurance. Thus the scene was set for romance, travel and – on the business scene – the prospect of an area of conflict.

At this stage we come upon something which to anyone concerned with the history of the Greigs represents a tremendous bonus. On all his worldwide travels throughout his working life, Walter Greig wrote copious letters home to his brothers, carbon copies of which he kept in notebooks. In them he describes not only his business activities in detail but also gives a zestful and colourful commentary on everything from geysers in New Zealand to the inadequacy and high cost of Cuban hotel rooms.

RMS *Orcoma*, on which the Greigs embarked on their six-month honeymoon and business trip in 1926.

The first and most fascinating of the notebooks begins with the 1926 tour. Datelined RMS *Orcoma* on 19.2.26, the first entry is a little sad for Mildred on her honeymoon: 'We sailed yesterday at 1 p.m. It seemed to take us all the rest of the day to get round Holyhead. This morning it is fine and some sun but it is a little rough. M keeps her bed but I hope she will soon get her sea legs.'

Next day, however, he was able to report that Mildred was better and had gone on deck and three days later she was 'very fit and now enjoying herself'. By then they were having warm sun in Corunna, where they had a look round the town and saw Sir John Moore's grave. Touchingly, he found that to have a travelling companion gave him new eyes: 'Yesterday we saw Santander which is a beautiful seaside place where the King of Spain has a Palace. Rocky shore and beautiful sands. Going on a trip like this with a companion is a very different affair from travelling alone and it being all new to M makes it interesting to me also.'

HONEYMOON

The Greigs' journey to New Zealand was to be by way of the Panama Canal, from where they had a passage booked to Auckland on the New Zealand Line ship *Remuera*. Their first business call, meanwhile, was at Havana where they arrived on 8 March, to be greeted by Señores de Zaldo and José Diaz of the Metropolitana – referred to by Walter as the Metro. The next forty-eight pages of his notes report on everything from burglary insurance and the fire risk involved in growing sugar cane to the Metro's treaties. 'The business ceded by the Metro to the REA,' he wrote on 14 March,

The Panama Canal as it would have appeared to the honeymoon couple as they passed through on the New Zealand Line ship Remuera en route *to Auckland.*

is very good for many reasons. Firstly Mr Diaz is a very good careful underwriter and secondly about 70 per cent of the Metro business covers risks in Havana and a large proportion of these cover buildings. The construction here is very good indeed. A large majority of the buildings have tile roofs and by this I mean the tiling you walk about on.

Motor conflagration, meanwhile, had caught his eye as a potentially interesting new source of business. The Metro, he noted, were looking for quotations for risks of this type:

This would cover garages, principally in Havana. The Metro write motor business very carefully. I think they have an income of about $30,000. They only insure cars in private ownership and do not accept old cars. They do the business very carefully and wish to be protected against the risk of being caught with a number of cars in one fire. I think they would pay 1 per cent and see no reason why the premium should be higher than in B[uenos] A[ires].

Most evenings there were dinners with the Metro underwriters and their wives, and several days of sightseeing, not to mention golf. In a long letter to his brother on the 14th, he adds a note of warning about his expenses: 'I do not wish to alarm you but I have just paid last week's hotel bill which was just about £53 and the hotel is very poor at that.'

Meanwhile the long-range aim of the New Zealand visit was not forgotten, for on the same page he recorded two chance encounters which evidently seemed like good omens for his coming meeting in Dunedin. 'Tomorrow we are going out with a Mr Rigg, the Royal Inspector and curiously enough his wife and Mr George Ritchie's wife are sisters. It is curious how we are meeting Mr Ritchie's friends. A lady on board the *Orcoma* knew the Ritchies well and had often been to their home in Dunedin.'

The next extended letter is dated 2 April, when the *Remuera* was four days out of Panama. For the next three weeks there was nothing but his fellow-passengers and the beauties of the Pacific to describe:

> *For the last two days we have been coming through the doldrums on a glassy sea without any more movement than that made by the movement of the ship ... It has been very hot indeed and the nights uncomfortable ... we are now making for Pitcairn Island on which live the descendants of the survivors of the mutineers of HMS* Bounty *... I am reading all I can about New Zealand. We are both very fit I am glad to say ... the Captain is giving us a lecture on Pitcairn Island tonight.*

But soon the long voyage is becoming irksome: 'We have seen no ship since leaving the American coast ... I am beginning to take an interest in business again,' he wrote on 13 April.

There was almost another week to go before the Greigs stepped onto dry land – at Auckland, where Walter, no doubt glad to see another insurance man again, called on Percy Upton of the South British. The same evening they travelled on to Wellington, arriving at 1.30 p.m. Indefatigable as ever, Walter took a professional stroll around the town: 'I did not have time to call on anyone so occupied myself studying the Town which is very important from our point of view owing to the earthquake risk. They have not had a serious earthquake there since 1850 or so but the place is always threatened ... It is a very beautiful place.'

From Wellington they travelled down to Dunedin where, on the 23rd, he called on Mr Mallard. 'We have not discussed business yet but he is being most kind ... He took us for two motor drives yesterday and is taking us for two today.' Meanwhile, Walter noted that he was to meet the board on Monday and that George Ritchie would be there for the discussions on the treaty. Mr Mallard and his daughter had taken the Greigs on yet more excursions, and there is typical magnanimity in Walter's attitude to his opponent:

He is most kind ... He is really against the whole system of Treaties. He is old fashioned. He knows however that they must keep up to date and I fear that if they do this business it will be a bitter pill for him and I am very sorry for him. I like him very much ... They may not do the business, however, then I shall probably be sorrier still. It seems to me that they must get treaties sooner or later and I hope Mr Mallard will be able to reconcile himself to it now.

Dunedin, New Zealand, in the early years of this century. Walter met here with the board of the National Insurance Company to discuss reciprocal reinsurance.

By the next entry in the notebook, on the 26th, the treaty situation was beginning to develop:

This is Monday and I have met the Board. It is arranged that I have preliminary discussions with Mr Mallard and Mr Birch ... Mr Ritchie was very nice and is asking us to dinner tomorrow. Mr Mallard told me he was afraid he might get a large amount at Wellington under the London Treaty. I may wire you for information regarding the amount at risk there.

But after a week, no progress had been made. With typical consideration, Walter had put in a word for the sergeant-cook: 'I have spoken up for Galbraith and if anything goes through I am seeing that he gets the kudos,' he wrote on the 28th, but when the following Monday went by with no decision, he began showing signs of irritation. The hotels, he noted, were very bad: he and Mildred had already had to change once. Meanwhile, he could make no plans until he knew the decision of the board. Mildred was hoping to see the famous Rotorua hot springs. 'I don't know if we can spare the three or so days there,' Walter wrote. 'It is a pity to come so far and not see the things of worldwide fame but we can't do everything.'

At last on 7 May, he had some real news:

We have had the momentous Board meeting. I explained the business and then Mr Mallard being pressed by the directors declared himself against it. The directors favour it, they were not impressed by his arguments but do not care to act against their executive. The matter was therefore adjourned till today ... Mr Mallard will not take a broad view. He fastens on certain arguments or facts which really have nothing to do with the business in question. For instance he says the Atlas underwriting excess for 3 or 4 years was 3 or 4 or 6 per cent, how therefore can their treaty be good, or the Eagle Star have had bad results owing to bad treaty results in Canada and America and all kinds of things of that nature.

The day of 8 May – Len's birthday, Walter noted as he inscribed the date – was the day that crowned his New Zealand efforts. 'All well,' his notebook entry reads, with evident relief, and he goes on to note that when his proposals for a treaty were put to the board, Mr Ritchie spoke up in person:

It was agreed that their treaty be placed in London against reciprocity which was to be very conservative in character ... Details such as the number of lines was left to Mr Mallard and me to decide ... He kindly congratulated me after the meeting on the attainment of my project. Since this really meant a victory over his old opinions I thought it very gentlemanly of him ... I am very thankful that the business has gone through for at one time it seemed very doubtful.

After the decisive board meeting there remained some details to be resolved, notably the cancellation of a treaty with the Samarang Insurance Company of Indonesia which had just been taken over by the Sun in London. There were also some reinsurance arrangements with other local companies which would need to be reviewed or cancelled in the light of the new treaty with the London market. Following these came Walter's decision to take a ten-day break to make a tour of the Southern Lakes and Mount Cook. 'I feel a little diffident about this trip,' he wrote to Kenneth, perhaps a shade guiltily since London was currently suffering the effects of the General Strike, 'but feel it is the right thing for many reasons. We have had a lot of travelling and staying in hotels more or less on the qui vive, dinner parties and teas, etc. I think ten days clean off duty would be a good thing.'

The Greigs left Dunedin on 13 May, beginning a ten-day tour during which they saw everything from volcanoes to snow-capped alps while also sampling Maori cooking. Walter had booked a passage from Auckland for Sydney on 4 June, and on 23 May they returned to Wellington to see Barry Simpson, the National Insurance Company's Manager, where Walter returned to the subject of the city blocks:

> It is a hazardous town certainly but the total sum reinsured is £66,000 so each reinsurer if there were eight lines would only have about £8,000 over the whole of Wellington. The reinsurers need not worry about Wellington ... the National write most carefully there. I have now to deal with the Australian faction. I expect and hope I shall have a busy fortnight and then for home.

In fact the Sydney visit was to be almost as momentous as the one to Dunedin. The Greigs arrived on 8 June, planning to return to England on the *Orvieto* three weeks later. The first few days were spent making or renewing social contacts – but by the 16th Walter had sensed that there was enough interest in reciprocal business from the United to make it worthwhile to stay on, and he decided to change their passages to the *Valdera*, the next England-bound ship. 'I am staying till the *Valdera*,' he wrote on the 25th, 'on account of the United. I do want to get a little further with that business if possible.'

Even then his key interview with the United did not take place until 2 July – two days before the ship sailed. 'We discussed reciprocal treaties fully,' Walter wrote later from the *Valdera*:

> I said we would place their business for nothing and only charge them

1½ per cent on the Treaties if the business went through their London office or 2½ per cent if we did the whole of the work. I propose a treaty of six lines as sufficient to start with. If the income was about £30,000 this would give a fair volume per line and the Treaty could be increased as regards lines if the income increased. They could not give up the local Facultative reinsurance.

The pattern might be familiar enough on Walter Greig's world tour, but for the United it was breaking new ground. Before then, as Douglas Rathbone recalled, anything more sophisticated than a one-off facultative reinsurance was unknown. 'Until that time,' he said,

Australia and New Zealand were so remote and under-developed from an insurance point of view that they didn't have a treaty at all, so a company like the United had no reinsurance arrangements. Every reinsurance they needed was done facultatively. If someone came in to the office to insure something starting today, and if the amount was bigger than they wanted – which was nearly always because retentions were very small – they immediately sent a clerk racing round central Sydney on a bicycle, placing £500 here and £500 there with a dozen other companies. That still existed for every pennyworth of their business till WT persuaded them to form a treaty. Greigs began to earn a lot more commission after the new business that he brought in on that tour.

CHAPTER FOUR

The inter-war years

The office of La Rosario, one of Walter Greig's important early clients in Buenos Aires (now the site of the Argentine finance house Leng Roberts – a landmark of the modern business centre)

When the *Valdera* docked at Tilbury in the last week of July 1926, it must have seemed to Walter Greig that he was on the threshold of a blossoming new world. Returning from his honeymoon tour, he had brought back a new book of business that would more than double the income from his existing contracts. Moreover, the omens for the worldwide insurance business were looking good. Premium income levels everywhere were increasing in the wake of the post-war economic boom. Everything suggested that he had picked the right moment to begin his new firm.

As a first step after Walter's return the brothers decided to take on more staff. They had already moved to larger premises in Royal Exchange Avenue, a tiny but attractive alley between Threadneedle Street and Cornhill. These modest expansions were followed by a new and ambitious business scheme involving Greigs and La Rosario: aimed at providing an agricultural all-risks cover that went considerably further than anything of its kind before, this was seen as a potential best-seller among Argentina's wealthy farming community, for whom it would give protection for the country's massive crop.

For the reinsurance of such a project there could be only one place – Lloyd's, the great insurance market which had begun life in a London coffee-house two and a half centuries before. Over more recent years its prestige as a marine insurance centre had dwindled somewhat, as the development of new companies began to threaten Lloyd's once-formidable monopoly of marine risks. As a result, the Lloyd's market – now housed a few steps away from Walter Greig's office – had begun to turn increasingly to non-marine. In this its leading spirit had been Cuthbert Heath, an admiral's son who had been unable to follow his father into the Navy because of his deafness. From the 1880s onwards, it had been Heath's inventiveness and readiness to write all kinds of new schemes that had given Lloyd's its reputation as somewhere where you could insure anything. In the field of reinsurance, it was Heath who, after the San Francisco earthquake, evolved the idea of

The inter-war years

excess of loss reinsurance to protect insurance companies from huge catastrophe claims.

Heath was in his late sixties and something of an elder statesman when Walter Greig went to see him over the La Rosario agricultural scheme, probably in C.E. Heath and Co.'s office in Royal Exchange Buildings, just round the corner from his own. What words passed on that occasion through Heath's famous ear-trumpet – he was said to hear or not hear according to what interested him – are sadly not known.

Sadder still, the new scheme did not work. The first and immediate disappointment was that the new agricultural policies failed to sell in anything like the numbers Walter and La Rosario had hoped: there was so little interest from the Argentine farmers that the profits earned by Greigs in 1927, the first year, came to £25. Worse was to come when the Argentine harvest suffered its worst-ever plague of wheat-rust. By the following year the volume of premium had climbed to a point where Greigs made a commission of £138 – but again the claims rolled in, this time because of an exceptionally severe drought. After a third year in which Greigs' commission was still under £300, the scheme was gradually wound down.

By now the horizon which had looked so promising on Walter Greig's return was beginning to look stormy. World economic conditions were moving ever closer to a slump. The drop in insured values, always an accurate indicator of the economy, meant less premium for the underwriters and so less commission for the brokers. In 1928 and 1929 the two new companies with whom Greigs had become involved, the United of Australia and the National of New Zealand, made booming profits on their reciprocal treaties – but from then on the profits began to decrease.

An autographed souvenir of a dinner in honour of Walter Greig held at the Conte Restaurant in Buenos Aires. It is signed by many of his associates at Leng Roberts.

The young Douglas Rathbone, who joined the company in 1928 at the age of 18 and was to become a leading figure and innovator in post-war reinsurance.

The year 1928 was to bring Greigs one piece of what was to remain for the next sixty years resoundingly good news. This was the arrival of an 18-year-old named Douglas Rathbone who, in later years, would be a guiding hand on the whole firm. For the moment, however, at a salary of £60 a year, he was an accounts clerk whose job was to check the mountainous sheets of reinsurance documents in the form of bordereaux which remained the bane of an insurance office.

For a young lad fresh from Selhurst Grammar School, the office routine meant making contact with romantic-sounding places across the world by means and messages that were often quite dull. Douglas Rathbone recalled that most days began with decoding cables, perhaps from La Rosario in Buenos Aires or the Credito Italiano in Rome, with the help of Bentley's green codebook with its five-letter codewords. Then there would come half an hour of delivering letters to other City offices by hand and, once a week, Rathbone remembered, he would send off the overseas mail. 'This,' he said, 'was because on Saturdays there was a regular mailship for Buenos Aires and one for Australia and New Zealand ... a letter to New Zealand could not receive a reply for about three and a half months and even the Argentine mail took seven or eight weeks.'

Meanwhile Walter Greig was continuing his world tours, as always demonstrating his ingenuity and versatility when it came to new kinds of business opportunities. December 1929 found him in Melbourne, looking at the possibilities raised by Mr Menzie of the Commercial of Australia for a cover which has the ring of our own time:

> *He wants to know a rate for insuring his new 12-storey building against malicious damage, i.e., a malicious person throwing a bomb at it. Someone threw a bomb at one of their insured premises the other day. The F[ederal] M[utual] are of course not liable for the damage done under a fire policy and the thought went through Menzie's mind that his client or a friend might come and throw a bomb against his building. The thing is most remote but if the rate were low they might think of it.*

Reading his notebooks, one is continually aware of his quick reaction to any form of new risk. In March 1932, he is talking to his Buenos Aires friends about 'accidents to passengers in aeroplanes ... I am to

The inter-war years

get from Heath details of policies covering Passengers in regular airlines.' A week later, the same subject comes up again:

> *La Rosario want details of policies covering air liners on established air routes. The principal concerns here are NYRBA [New York–Rio–Buenos Aires]. I take it that policies could be reinsured under the All Risks contract but La Rosario would like details of policies, proposal forms and rates used in England. Roberts for instance is going to fly to Madagascar when he next goes and would certainly take a policy. There are many like this and there have been many enquiries.*

But by now such items were beginning to be little more than flashes of optimism against the darkening economic gloom. Premium, following commodity values, was declining fast: over the four years between 1929 and 1933, the total commission earned by Greigs went down by over 28 per cent. All the large British companies were showing losses on their reinsurance treaties – one contributory cause being the tragically high incidence of arson losses, the result of desperate businessmen trying to avoid ruin by making fraudulent claims.

When, in March 1933, Walter Greig set off on his usual spring journey to South America, it was beginning to look as if the firm might soon find itself in crisis. The London companies' results were about to be announced – and if 1932 was going to turn out as bad as the previous few years, there was a strong chance that the Argentine companies would no longer want to participate in the reciprocal treaties on which Greigs' fortunes were so largely based. And if, as seemed more than possible, the Australian and New Zealand companies were to follow suit, it could mean the end of Walter Greig's dream.

Havana in the 1920s, when Walter and Mildred Greig visited the city.

The top hat worn by Walter Greig in his early City years, now kept in its original box beside his son John's desk at Devon House.

But luck had always favoured him and now, at what was certainly the most critical moment in the firm's history so far, his luck held. For just as he was stopping off at Havana on his way to the crucial Buenos Aires meeting, it so happened that Kenneth Greig, in London, happened to call on B.B. Fisher, as the Foreign Fire Manager of the Royal Exchange Assurance was known to all his London friends and colleagues in those pre-first name days. Astonishingly, B.B. Fisher assured Kenneth Greig, the Royal Exchange results looked like doing well for the first time for four years. B.B. Fisher himself said he found it hard to believe, but a 10 per cent profit seemed probable for the 1932 year.

Kenneth's immediate reaction was to cable the good news to Walter in Havana, where he was having what had been expected to be gloomy conversations about reciprocal deals with his old friend, José Diaz. Walter's delight was unconcealed in the cable he sent back:

It seems too good to be true but the wording of your cable leaves no doubt that 1932 results of REA business will give a profit of 8 per cent at least and this of course makes all the difference in talking to Diaz. Their income from the REA is about £18,000 and there is another £7,000 in the Unión Nacional, which makes a profit of about £2,000 in 1932 ... As I say, it seems too good to be true, I cannot say how pleased I am ... I take it you have advised Buenos Aires to give you an extra bit of their treaty from La Rosario. Last year's results should have a favourable effect towards influencing La Rosario to accepting it.

Amazingly, over the next week or so, the Royal Exchange figures were reflected in all the other London company results – and one consequence was a sudden call for more reciprocal fire reinsurance treaties, which continued to be profitable from then until after the Second World War.

What was the reason for the sudden sea change? Why, when the odds seemed all against them, did the London companies go back to making profits? The answer, tantalisingly, is that no one knows. Even Douglas Rathbone, who was close to the events of the time, had no explanation of why things turned out as they did. 'The contrast with the previous year is so great it's still a mystery to me,' he said. 'But it was crucial to Greigs. Without it we might well have gone down.'

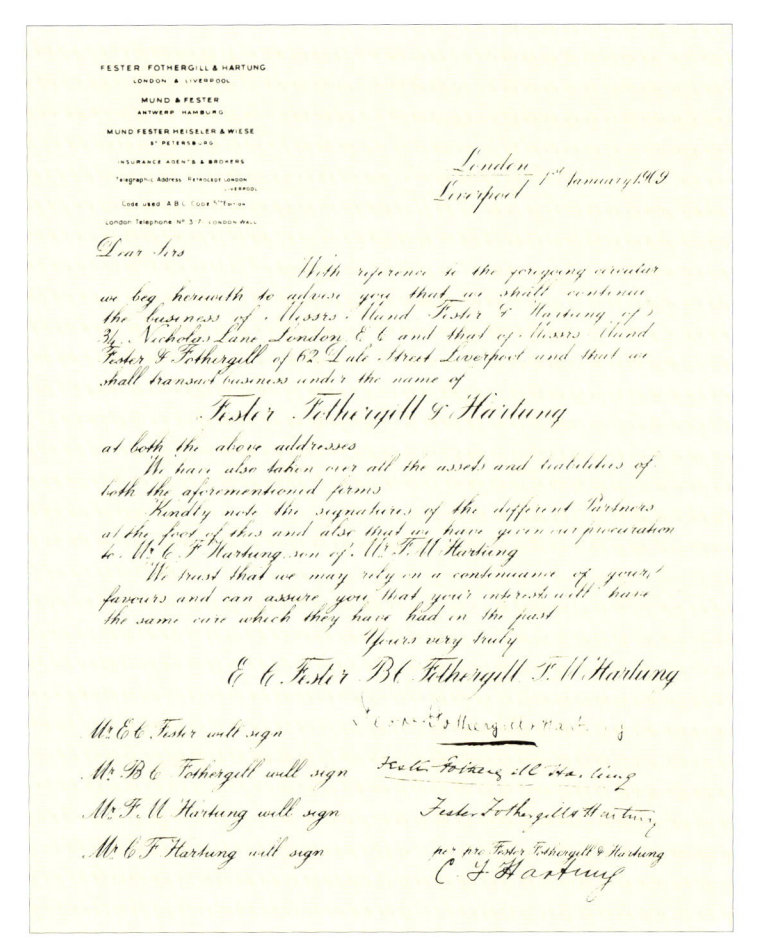

Letter announcing the merger in 1909 of Mund, Fester & Hartung of London with Mund, Fester & Fothergill of Liverpool. Together they formed the new partnership of Fester, Fothergill & Hartung.

Meanwhile, how had Fester, Fothergill & Hartung been faring? The year 1909, where we left them, had seen the merger of the London and Liverpool broking houses: later in the same year, there had come the death of Frederick Hartung, whose share of the company passed to his son, Carl Frederic. In 1910 Festers became a Lloyd's broker and also moved from Nicholas Lane – thus missing by eleven years being neighbours of the Greigs – to Suffolk House in Laurence Pountney Lane, the other side of Cannon Street.

The Fester partners, as depicted in a memoir by Archibald Errol who joined the firm in 1915, seem to have been hardly memorable. Emil Fester, the son of Heinrich Fester of Antwerp, was, according to Errol, a bon viveur 'who lived always in the grand style. His expensive trips to New York and Japan were the despair of his fellow partners. He considered himself the senior partner. His complaint was that the firm was not simply known as Festers.'

Next came Carl Frederic Hartung, described as 'extremely pleasant and likeable'. But Errol also gently notes that his 'kindly nature and generosity led him into frequent difficulties', which included an unwise investment in a goldmine from which he had to be rescued by his fellow-partners. Finally there was Basil Fothergill, always regarded as having been helped into the firm through his father's influence as General Manager of the London & Lancashire; he was, says Errol, 'a placid and kindly gentleman, usually in morning dress … he had little to do with the firm and it was the general opinion that his intelligence was rather limited, but in fact he was rather shrewder than was thought'.

The inter-war years

The company itself seems to have been run on relatively humane lines. 'There was a general friendliness and a really tremendous feeling of loyalty ... a great reluctance to dismiss anyone, however unsatisfactory. They were always to be given another chance,' says Errol – though he notes there was no pension scheme in those post-1914 war days.

Over these years Festers was gradually building up what would in the future be seen as key links. As far back as 1904 had come the beginning of one of Festers' most productive partnerships, with the First Bohemian Reinsurance Bank of Prague. In 1917 came the first contact with Japan through the Kyodo company, which would be added to in 1931 when one of Emil Fester's allegedly extravagant overseas trips paid off handsomely by producing another key contact with the Nissan. Important domestic changes included the arrival in 1922 of Harry Farmer who, over the next three decades, would increasingly come to be seen as guiding Festers' fortunes. Two years later came a move to the beautiful Rectory House (now demolished) at the north end of Southwark Bridge. Formerly the rectory of the Wren church of St Mary Aldermary, it was to remain their home for over four decades.

Harry Farmer, the guiding spirit behind Festers' growth and success in the years following the Second World War.

There was little to report from Greigs as Europe lurched from slump to world war. Earnings from brokerage continued to be modest, bringing the three partners a steady total of around £4,800 a year. Walter would go round visiting the companies if there was new business to be placed, or seeing old friends. When things were quiet, as they often were, the brothers would lunch at the City Carlton Club: when they returned, an hour spent reading *The Times* was not unusual. Greigs was not yet accredited to Lloyd's, so that an order for a facultative reinsurance would mean a phone call to a friendly broker who would observe the Lloyd's formalities by introducing Walter at a leading underwriter's box. 'By then the big reinsurance arrangements had all been set up,' recalled Douglas Rathbone. 'I don't believe that in any important respect there were half a dozen changes over ten years.'

The coming of war brought fire and destruction to the Square Mile, but for many people in the insurance business life simply went on. Greigs was among the firms who decided to evacuate their office and,

The Tokyo earthquake of 1923, a significant event in the development of earthquake insurance in Japan.

THE INTER-WAR YEARS

on 1 September 1939, the firm's papers and account books were moved down to Walter's house at Kingswood, Surrey, in the guard's van of a London Bridge train. For the next two years the firm functioned from the Greigs' table-tennis room, to the satisfaction of everyone except the present Chairman, John Greig, then an 8-year-old schoolboy who missed his table-tennis table. His sister Elspeth, a schoolgirl at the time, recalls the experience as being 'all harmonious and very pleasant … There was Douglas Rathbone, with whom my mother got on very well, and two or three other people. They used to bring their packed lunches and eat them sitting in the sun.'

In 1942 Greigs decided to move back to London. Making the most of the readily available office space, they took over the second floor of a spacious building at No. 14 Cornhill. Festers, who had evacuated to Cromer in August 1939, soon found the transport and postal problems insuperable – 'the post office were unused to telegrams to Japan', writes Errol – and were back in London after two months.

The Second World War made little impact on Greigs as a company. Festers, on the other hand, was in a very different position because a great deal of its business was placed in Europe. Dealings with a country with whom Britain is at war are traditionally banned by the Trading with the Enemy Act, which comes into force the moment war is declared or a country is occupied: at the start of the Second World War, it had seemed likely that only business with Germany, Austria, Poland and perhaps Italy would be affected. But in 1940, as the Nazi war machine rolled west, the law applied in turn to Norway, Belgium, The Netherlands, France – and eventually, barring only Switzerland, Spain, Sweden and Portugal, to the whole of Europe. This time the

In September 1939, Greigs relocated to Walter and Mildred's home at Kingswood, Surrey, avoiding the devastation which hit the City's Square Mile in the early years of the War. The firm operated from Kingswood for over two years, moving back to the City in 1942.

London market had made considerably better arrangements than in the First World War. What were known as shadow contracts had been set up. These meant that, for instance, a French company might be replaced by a Canadian one on a reinsurance treaty: when trade with France was prohibited, the French company was automatically replaced. As a result of the war, Festers lost out considerably because so many of the treaties arranged were with companies in Europe. Greigs, however, was often in a position to find, for instance, a South American or Australian company to replace a European one.

A tailpiece to the story of Greigs in the war came when Douglas Rathbone, by then an officer with HMS *Indefatigable*, spent December 1944 in Sydney, his ship's home port. Here he made the most of the opportunity of renewing relationships with many of Greigs' Australian clients. Later, after taking part in the Battle of Okinawa, his ship had gone on to Japanese seas, being only a hundred miles from Tokyo when the surrender of August 1945 came. At that point Douglas Rathbone would normally have been demobilised, but instead he accepted an invitation to stay on for a series of goodwill tours in Australia. Cheerfully dividing an eighteen-hour working day between the Admiralty and Greigs, he was able to meet almost all the company's clients in the southern hemisphere.

As a location, it could hardly have been more appropriate. For in the great changes that Greigs was to bring to the reinsurance scene, Australia was to play a key part.

CHAPTER FIVE

Innovation and change

The aftermath of the 1954 Adelaide earthquake

The London to which the servicemen and women returned in 1945 was in many ways a new world. True, it would be a long time before the war-torn city would be rebuilt: as yet the sky-line east of Temple Bar had no taller buildings than the Monument and St Paul's dome. But the tempo of life had speeded up: the copperplate written by pre-war clerks was rarely to be seen, while business trips by air replaced the sea-voyages that before the war had taken three months. In subtler ways there were changes in the manners of the times, with office colleagues beginning to call each other by their first names for the first time. Nor was it only an effect of the new Labour government that class barriers seemed to be coming down, so that young men who had achieved rapid promotion in the services were no longer content to wait for their supervisors to retire, but sought to carve out new careers for themselves in double-quick time.

A 'morning after' view of damage caused by the Blitz, looking towards London Bridge from the Guardian Assurance building. Regis House, later to become Greig Fester's head office for seventeen years, is on the left.

The two decades after the war were to bring greater changes to the London insurance market than it had seen throughout its long life. Some of these would be the result of events within the industry itself – such as the growing strength of great companies in Munich, Zurich and New York. Others were the effect of broader political change – notably the rise of the new nations of what was becoming known as the Third World. For many of these, insurance and especially reinsurance was a means of earning not only premium but also international prestige. By the 1960s, as one experienced observer of the London market, Jim Bannister, has pointed out, the new entrants to reinsurance were coming from 'medium-size and large insurers who thought they could build a profitable account on the back of their own outwards placing; state reinsurers formed to avoid the loss of foreign exchange; captive insurers who had made money writing their own business, and a host of others who thought reinsurance was an easy way to make money'. All this meant that London brokers began to find themselves in a new role. In the past, the world had come to London to buy its insurance. But in the new situation, the travelling was being done by the broker and the risks that had once been placed direct in London were now coming back as reinsurance.

There was also, notably, the tendency to merge. The post-war years saw the formation of huge composite companies whose constituents had often, not long before, been ten or twelve distinct firms. All this affected the reinsurers profoundly too, for as the companies grew larger and wealthier, they could afford to retain more and to reinsure less. Big companies, however, could become victims of their size. The insurance industry had always been notorious as a builder of paper mountains, but in the 1950s and 1960s its administrative costs soared.

In 1945 much of this still lay in the future of the market. At Greigs, the immediate post-war years had brought little sign of change. Reciprocal treaties were still the mainstay, often with the same clients of twenty years ago. Walter Greig, now 61, still came to the office every day, but limited his overseas travel to an annual sea-voyage to Buenos Aires. The reins of the company were gradually moving into Douglas Rathbone's hands: made a director in 1948, he set off on the first air journey made by a member of the Greig staff, visiting India, New Zealand and Australia, where he managed to persuade the United to have all their marine cargo reinsurances centred in a single excess of loss contract – a deal which within four months had earned twice the commission of any contract Greigs had handled up to that date.

It was a significant pointer to some of the new kinds of reinsurances that were to come – but meanwhile Walter Greig was to provide one last, brilliant example of his negotiating skills. This came when the new Perón regime in Argentina announced its intention of nationalising reinsurance. Known as IMAR (Instituto Mixto Argentino de

WALTER T. GREIG

Innovation and change

Reaseguros), the new national company was jointly owned by the government and the existing companies. From then on, the law would be that the companies would have to cede all their fire and marine risks to IMAR.

Walter Greig was quick to see that this would be a disastrous blow, not only for Greigs but also for the London companies who valued their profitable fire business from Argentina. So why, Walter suggested, should IMAR not create a new mechanism by which the exchanges could still go on? For a start, he told the London companies, all the exchanges could be continued against an IMAR retrocession.

Having obtained their agreement, he went to Buenos Aires where, after weeks of delicate diplomacy, he persuaded IMAR that it would be in their interests to set up a fire treaty to serve as a reciprocal vehicle for the exchanges. By 1948, the new arrangement was in place, though the full scope of Walter Greig's achievement was not seen until four years later, when IMAR became INDER (Instituto Nacional de Reaseguros) and a full government monopoly. By then 23 per cent of the company's principal fire treaty was being managed by Greigs.

In the library at Devon House there is a wall-map showing the areas of the world most liable to earthquakes. Particularly eye-catching is the fringe of fire which runs jaggedly down the west coast of the USA and on to Chile. Across the Pacific runs its counterpart, a similar fiery rim down the east Asian coast, through Japan and then south to New Zealand. Another destructive trail runs west to the Black Sea, then on through Greece and Italy to north Africa.

The wall-map which hangs in the library at Devon House, showing the earthquake zones of the world. Greig Fester have continued to show interest in the scientific prediction of natural disasters.

Earthquakes and reinsurance could be called two sides of a coin, for in the end the cost of these disaster-trails are paid by reinsurers. Cuthbert Heath, in his earliest days at Lloyd's, compiled an 'earthquake book' which included notes on disasters as far back as the fifteenth century made by Jesuit missionaries on the west coast of north America. In Heath's own time, the risks had been written extensively at Lloyd's, where the underwriters would often charge as much as 40 per cent of the sum insured for a year's premium to reinsure the earthquakes that assailed America's west coast – the same applying to their twins, the windstorms that blew up from the Caribbean along its east coast.

But outside Lloyd's the writing of catastrophe risks was still almost unknown: Greigs only had one such piece of business on the books, from the New Rotterdam Insurance Company, as late as 1951. The reason was that while the companies covering the USA felt they needed to reinsure, those in Britain, New Zealand and Australia bought little or no catastrophe cover because there were so few claims. 'We don't get catastrophes in Australia,' Greigs was told by one general manager from Sydney in the late 1940s. They were words that would ring ironically in due course.

But Douglas Rathbone had always sensed that there might one day be possibilities for Greigs in the reinsurance of these risks, and the thought came back when, one day in 1951, he was lunching with Reg Wetherley, the Northern Assurance Company Ltd's underwriter. 'He told me he had managed to persuade his general manager to let him write some catastrophe reinsurance,' Rathbone recalled. 'From then on, we started seeking orders from companies who were interested in some modest catastrophe cover if it could be bought at very cheap rates.' As a result of the meeting, the Northern, and soon other companies, began writing the risks at a fraction of the Lloyd's rate – justifiably, as it seemed, because of the apparently low risk.

Among those who responded most rapidly to the possibilities of the new market were Festers. Through the 1950s they had developed close and important links with the Norwich Union, for whom they handled many reciprocal exchanges. One area of special concern was Jamaica, which is exposed to catastrophe risks of both windstorms and earthquakes, and it is not a bad example of the international nature of the reinsurance business that Festers placed an important catastrophe cover for the Norwich Union's Jamaica account with the Aequitas Re of Gothenburg in Sweden.

In 1954 came an event which was to speed the expansion of the new market in catastrophe covers outside Lloyd's. On 1 March the city of Adelaide was rocked by an earthquake whose shocks were felt in the surrounding countryside 200 miles off. Apart from the extensive damage to offices and homes, there were cracks in Government House and other civic buildings which the Queen was to visit on the forthcoming royal tour.

Fortunately no one was killed, but the Adelaide earthquake had come as an unpleasant warning. 'Since the turn of the year,' *The Times* business correspondent wrote on 6 March,

> *Australia has had the unhappy experience of floods, storms and earth tremors. Flood cover is seldom given by insurers ... On the other hand the claims under comprehensive policies covering dwellings are likely to be numerous as a result ... of the storm which struck the coast of southern Queensland and northern New South Wales on February 20 and the earth tremor in South Australia on March 1 ... Such losses ... are a reminder that exceptional fire and storm experiences are among the risks that insurers have to be prepared for from time to time; and during the last year or so Nature would seem to have been more liberal of such experiences than for some time.*

The Adelaide earthquake could be said to have given the fledgling catastrophe market a slight push. Even so, it was to be several years yet before catastrophe reinsurance began to replace the proportional treaty business which would remain Greigs' staple fare. John Andrews, a former Northern underwriter who joined in 1972, recalls that even then 'the reciprocal treaty side was still of enormous importance to profits ... One exchange developed a premium of £1 million each way, and in those days a great number of cat[astrophe] contracts were needed to match the £30,000 odd of brokerage of this one single relationship.'

One of the features of the post-war insurance market was the way it had become top heavy with administration, with the result that the companies were seeking ways to cut costs. At the same time the mergers of the 1950s had helped to create giant composites, often with massive reserves of capital. One effect of this was that they began to look for ways in which they might retain more premium by reinsuring less.

All this was in Douglas Rathbone's mind when, one afternoon in 1961, he was visited in London by an Australian insurance man named Jack Williams, the General Manager of the United in Sydney, one of Walter Greig's clients. The London companies might have their administrative problems, but the United's were worse still: he had the reinsurance of thousands of small houses on his surplus treaties. Every single risk had to be calculated separately for, like many of the Australian and New Zealand companies at the time, he was retaining very small sums, geared to such parochial questions as the nearness of fire services to a particular house, and whether or not it had a wooden frame, and was therefore a worse risk.

Because of these varying retentions and the amount of small detail involved, Williams' problem was an extreme case. But Douglas Rathbone realised that if Greigs could not find the solution to his problem, someone else would – which would mean losing one of Greigs' best clients.

That evening he went home to Croydon, had supper and, as usual on a summer evening, worked in his garden.

> *I turned the earth over and I turned the problem over too. After I'd been working for about half an hour I suddenly thought: any one risk. With surplus treaties, every single risk had to be separately recorded and it was very laborious. But if he could retain £500 – say about three-quarters of the value of each house – as his first loss on each risk separately, then I could sell the excess of any claim over £500 for a fraction of 1 per cent in the London market. The result was that Williams got all his tens of thousands of houses insured in a single contract without any calculations.*

Why was this so much better for the ceding company? In the first place, it enabled them to keep more premium, which was their first aim, for now that they were getting larger and richer there was less and less point in their reinsuring the very small risks. All their general managers needed in order to sleep soundly was the knowledge that their reinsurers were taking care of the larger risks.

Innovation and change

Nearly as important to them was the saving in paperwork and administration. Under the old surplus treaties, the ceding company had to keep records of every risk and calculate the proportion of premium for each one separately. The new contract meant that they only had to do a simple calculation once a quarter to work out the percentage of premium required by the reinsurer.

On Douglas Rathbone's next visit to New Zealand, the National Insurance Company brought up a problem that was similar to, but not quite the same as that of the United. 'They were looking for a policy to be applied to their whole portfolio of fire business,' he recalled. 'The suggestion was that what previously had been a cover for small dwellings should now be extended to the company's whole commercial and industrial portfolio.' The result of his New Zealand talks was that Greigs was able to place contracts in the London market covering all risks except the very biggest.

The companies were quick to realise that the new any one risk covers would enable them to retain more premium and to keep administrative costs down. Many of the new policies were led by Gustav Grabscheid of the Guardian, a close associate of Douglas Rathbone and a brilliant reinsurance man who had left Vienna before the war, entered the insurance business in London and risen to the point where he was now seen as a market leader. Soon other brokers were paying Greigs the compliment of copying this new idea. It became a best-seller and has continued to be one ever since.

There was another variation on the theme of any one risk. The obvious snag for the ceding companies was that, happy as they were to retain more of their premium, they were less happy to be responsible for the large amounts of retained catastrophe risks they might be accumulating. So what they did next was to turn to the new company catastrophe market which had begun with Douglas Rathbone's lunch with the Foreign Fire Manager of the Northern. For the ceding companies, the good news was that the cost of the catastrophe reinsurance was only a fraction of the premium income that the any one risk scheme had enabled them to claw back. It was far cheaper from the companies' point of view to buy any one risk and the new kind of catastrophe reinsurance than buying the surplus treaties.

Meanwhile Douglas Rathbone, now at the height of his inventive powers, was to launch yet another new scheme. This time it related to one of those areas which seem to take insurance almost to the edge of higher mathematics: the problem of how to define, in terms of a contract which pays a loss on 'any one event', what the one event is. When an earthquake could do damage over several hours, where does the event begin and end? Douglas Rathbone, seeking to design a cover for Australian companies insuring against bushfire risks, quickly saw that the client's essential requirement was protection from all the bushfires that might happen.

So he drafted a clause in which 'one event' was to be the total of all claims in a season. 'The argument,' he pointed out, 'is that the real cause of the fire is the long, hot, dry summer. Several bushfires will happen at different places or at several times in the same place, but they will all come from the one cause.' Thus the annual aggregate bushfire clause, as it was called, became the norm in Australia and notably increased the amount of catastrophe cover which Greigs handled there.

Indeed the whole first half of the 1960s had seen important pioneering work from Greigs. Both the any one risk cover and the bushfire clause had created something of a market stir – while the tendency was steadily growing to link catastrophe insurance with their name. The background to this new emphasis was a trend which would later bring about a great change. Before the Second World War, few domestic policies covered the more dramatic areas of windstorm, earthquake, riots and floods – but by the 1960s, it was becoming commonplace for an ordinary householder's fire policy to cover these risks. One consequence of this was that people in general became much more aware of their ability to claim – while for householders whose homes would be wrecked by such events as the East Coast floods or the 1987 hurricane, the new cover became very good news.

From the earliest days Greigs could be said to have developed in three phases, each characterised, even dominated, by one man. Walter Greig was certainly the first, and we might call him the Traveller – both as an itinerant broker and for the sheer delight he took in the world around him. Reading his notebooks, one often senses that his business was at least partly a means by which he might more thoroughly enjoy life.

Since 1945 the company had been moulded by another strong man

Innovation and change

Douglas Rathbone

– this time the Selhurst schoolboy who had won himself a junior job and gone on to become a leading figure in post-war reinsurance. We might call this period the time of the Inventor, for during the 1950s and 1960s it was to Douglas Rathbone's innovations that Greigs owed much of the new fame that the company enjoyed.

The third leader was cast in a different mould again. But like the other two, he was precisely the right and dominating figure for his own time. So far we have met John Greig only as a schoolboy who missed his table-tennis room. But from the 1950s on, we are going to see his intellectual leadership transforming what had been a respected but modest family business into a company now famous worldwide.

John Greig has said that if he had not gone into the insurance business he would have thought of architecture as a career, and, following the Traveller and the Inventor, the Architect would seem the right symbol for him. For the great difference between him and his predecessors is that in their earlier, perhaps easier time, the company just naturally grew – whereas his more difficult role has been consciously to design, then build, the structure in a new form.

John Greig first came to work full time in 1950, when as much as a quarter of the firm's business was still with Argentina. Other Latin American countries were the domain of Denys Robinson, originally a Festers' broker, who had developed an account of his own in Mexico and travelled extensively throughout the Spanish-speaking countries.

Robinson's departure in 1955 meant that John Greig now took over the responsibility for the romantic roll call of countries that included Mexico, Venezuela, Colombia, Chile, Peru and Argentina. For a young man in his mid-twenties few things could have been more exhilarating than spending six weeks in Buenos Aires in the dramatic days of Perón. Often there would be complex negotiations to be done, requiring both diplomacy and the language skills he had learnt from Walter – while his weekends would bring visits to *estancias* outside the city. 'I was originally sent out,' John Greig recalls,

> *not only to get to know the people and to learn about the business, but incidentally to encourage them to despatch their treaty accounts more punctually. The result however was that they taught me that* mañana *was a useful word and that a coffee or a* clarito *in the local bar was not without its virtues when it came to doing business.*

Innovation and change

South America might up to this point seem to have played a disproportionately large part in Greigs' world. Soon the emphasis would be on much more expansion overseas: an Australian company was formed in 1957 which would later, under the leadership of John Allison, become a bright jewel in the Greig crown. There were to be other ventures into interesting new territories as well, and we shall return to these after an overdue look at what was happening at Festers.

Until 1945 the company had had to contend with the difficulty of holding many contracts not only with German companies, but also in other European countries excluded by the war rules. The same applied to Japan, where Festers had had active business relations since the First World War. After 1950 the relationship with the Kyodo company (now part of the Dowa) could be resumed.

Festers' income had begun to increase steadily through the post-war years. From £5,000 in 1949 it rose to £8,000 in 1951 – indeed by 1960 it was £100,000, more than Greigs earned in the same year. Much of this success was due to Harry Farmer who, over the immediate post-war years, had masterminded Festers' reciprocal trading with Japan as soon as the American occupation laws permitted. Through the original contact with the Kyodo company he was introduced to the Kyoei Mutual, and thus began placing the first post-war cessions of the much sought-after fire treaty business for three major companies, the Dowa, Nissan and Kyoei Mutual. Soon Festers was handling 173 reciprocal exchanges on behalf of their Japanese clients.

Besides this success in the Far East, important French deals had been secured in the form of motor insurance covers for two well-known companies, La Providence and La Préservatrice. Nearer home, however, the company was facing some uneasy problems. One was a threat to its relationship with the London & Lancashire, with which very strong links had always been maintained. For many years, Festers had been one of only two brokers that the company employed, and a large part of the reciprocal fire treaties had been handled through them.

So Festers' concern can be imagined when, towards the end of 1958, the market learned that the London & Lancashire was to be taken over by another northern company, the Royal. The news could hardly have been worse. The Royal, the nation's leading composite, was noted for the fact that, apart from a fire treaty for its overseas business, it had bought no treaty reinsurance since the first war. The same policy, the Royal announced, would now apply to the London & Lancashire. The year 1959 would see the disappearance of all its existing treaties.

It was Harry Farmer who had been responsible for almost all the company's post-war strengths. He died in 1958, but five years before, anxious to secure the company's prospects for the future, he had seen to the quick promotion to partnership of two promising and energetic young men. One was Brian Wallas, who had joined as a law graduate from Oxford in 1950: descended from Graham Wallas, one of the founders of the Fabian Society, he was, ironically enough, the son of the former general manager of the London & Lancashire whose takeover was to lead to the 1958 crisis. The other new arrival at Festers in the early 1950s had been Duncan Allen, a former Welsh Guards officer who had won an MC in north Africa.

In 1958, as it began to look more and more certain that £1 million worth of premium income was going to be lost, it fell to Wallas and Allen to see if there might not be some alternative way out. Over the months before the Royal's takeover, they began to seek every possible means of finding new partners for the overseas companies – they ranged from Europe and Venezuela to Japan – who until then had had reciprocal arrangements with the London & Lancashire. Sometimes the two young brokers would approach one former partner and suggest a deal with another: when the company had been seeing business with one firm in Mexico and another one in Holland, they tried setting up a contact between the Mexicans and Dutch. Thus they built up a whole new structure of exchanges. In the end, the threatened £1 million loss came down to a manageable £50,000 – while Festers had found a whole new range of clients.

1958 was also the year in which Frank Gill, who was later to become Manager and ultimately a Partner in Festers, joined the company after having gained reinsurance experience at another Lloyd's broking house. As a result of this new appointment, the story of the London & Lancashire received a new twist a year or so later. Festers decided to take a chance in breaking down the Royal's traditional resistance to reinsurance and after much skilful and persistent broking managed to

Brian Wallas

Frank Gill

INNOVATION AND CHANGE

persuade them to take an excess cover on their overseas accounts – a deal made possible by Brian Wallas and Frank Gill, who had encouraged the reinsuring company, the Northern, to take the business cheaply on the basis that it was a very safe risk. 'It was a big breakthrough for us to have obtained the Royal's first-ever excess of loss cover,' Brian Wallas recalls. 'In due course they became our number one client.'

But the ironic sequel came when, after everything that had been said about how safe the risk was going to be, the Royal found themselves collecting a loss of £300,000 from their reinsurers on Tasmanian bushfires before the cover had run twelve months.

In 1963, Greigs took a step which is something like the graduation of a broker: becoming one of the select list of those accredited to Lloyd's. At the same time, the company was recruiting some notably talented new staff. Take, for example, three unusually energetic young men who came to the company around the early 1960s, each with a style and skill of his own at selling the kind of high powered reinsurance in which Greigs dealt. John Merison was a former Fleet Air Arm officer who had suffered appalling back injuries after crashing in the Irish Sea. Outgoing, larger than life and vastly kind, he was the driving force in Greigs' foreign sales team. Next came Dieter Losse, a Cambridge graduate and brilliant linguist who had joined Greigs from the Swiss Re because he liked the idea of working in a small firm.

John Merison

Third in the triumvirate was Peter Keats, a kinsman of the poet, who had already worked in reinsurance when he came to Greigs in 1963. When he came out of the Navy, where he had served with HMS *Indefatigable* – Douglas Rathbone's old ship – he had been employed by C.E. Golding & Co., another long-established reinsurance brokers. He was particularly attracted to reinsurance broking because he wished to travel. Goldings had sent him to learn German by working with the Munich Re, but beyond that had offered him no further chance of travel. Peter Keats had answered an advertisement for a travelling broker put in the insurance press by Greigs, and had been interviewed in German by John Greig who asked if he was prepared to learn Spanish. Keats had agreed he would, but had been working at the language for only six months when he went on his first trip to

Dieter Losse

John Greig (left) recruited Peter Keats for the company's Latin American operations. Here they take time out in Mexico City, during Peter Keats' first overseas trip on company business in 1963.

Latin America. Nevertheless, the language came with the travel as he went to what he calls the 'earthquake countries' of Mexico, Nicaragua, Guatemala, Venezuela and Ecuador selling catastrophe reinsurance, gradually taking over from John Greig as the latter began to spend more and more time running the company in London.

While Peter Keats was selling reinsurance to the earthquake lands of Latin America, Dieter Losse's memories of journeys with John Merison to the East sound like merchants travelling to Bokhara rather than modern businessmen selling reciprocal or any one risk. 'We'd pack our bags and be off to Pakistan or the Middle East or the Far East. Sometimes we'd be on the road for three months at a stretch. It was very hard work, looking for business – any kind of business we could lay our hands on.'

John Merison's own speciality was Japan, which he had been visiting since 1950, often coinciding in the bar of Tokyo's Imperial Hotel with Brian Wallas, travelling for Festers. Dieter Losse felt privileged when John Merison asked him to go to help him there in his first year:

> *Normally people would reckon that you had to travel to Japan regularly for at least two years before you even got sight of a piece of business. But John's father had been managing director of a leading broker and his name was well known. But above all there was something about his personality that they took to, and he was able to accelerate things.*

Two of John Merison's acquaintances in Tokyo were to play a special part in smoothing Greigs' way. One was Tamotsu Hashimoto, the venerable President of the Toa Fire and Marine Reinsurance Co. (Toa Re) who, says Dieter Losse, 'was like a godfather to John. Most unusually for a Japanese, he was married to an Englishwoman who had

INNOVATION AND CHANGE

SUMMARY OF W.T. GREIG LTD INCOME ANALYSIS 1963

Territory	Number of sources	Totals £ s d	%
Australia	22	42,705. 7. –.	34.8
New Zealand	3	27,941. 9. 9.	22.7
Argentina	12	15,736.10.10.	12.8
UK	17	9,825.17. 7.	8.0
South Africa	2	6,338. 1. 9.	5.2
Pakistan	2	6,260. 7. 3.	5.1
Eire	3	2,285.13.10.	1.9
Philippines	6	2,070. 4. –.	1.7
India	8	1,588. 8. 2.	1.3
Japan	3	1,264. 0. 9.	1.0
Holland	5	1,120.10. 6.	0.9
Thailand	4	620. 4. 1.	0.5
Canada	2	420. 4. 9.	0.3
Sweden	2	391. 7. –.	0.3
Egypt	3	285. 3. 8.	0.2
Venezuela	1	248.11.10	0.2
Peru	1	142. 1. 2.	0.1
Spain	1	80. 9. 5.	0.1
Germany	1	50.17. –.	0.1
Panama	1	50. 1. 9.	0.1
Mexico	1	33.12. 7.	0.0
USA	1	21. 5. 8.	0.0
Columbia	2	37. 6. 8.	0.0
West Indies	1	20. 7. 8.	0.0
Malaya	2	19.19. –.	0.0
Mauritius	1	14. 2.11	0.0
Greece	1	13. 9. 6.	0.0
Norway	1	3. –. –.	0.0
Unaccounted for	–	8.12. –.	0.0
Miscellaneous currency (Adjt)	–	3,313.8. 4.	2.7
TOTAL	**109**	**£122,910.16. 5**	**100.0**

adapted to Japanese ways.' John Merison's other Tokyo friend was Geoffrey Hudson, an Englishman whose life had followed a strange path. Working for the Norwich Union, he had been sent by them in the 1930s to Shanghai. He had met Mr Hashimoto while in Japan, and then in Singapore had met and married the daughter of a major figure in local banking and insurance.

Captured after the fall of Singapore, Hudson had been put in the notorious Changi prison; when peace came, the Norwich Union sent him to their Paris branch to help him recuperate after the harrowing experience of Changi. But Hudson's feelings for the Japanese had not changed. He returned to Tokyo as head of the British Insurance Group, in due course meeting up again with his old friend Tamotsu Hashimoto. Hudson at this stage undertook a key role from the Japanese point of view, for he played a very considerable part in persuading General MacArthur, who was effectively President Truman's emissary in post-war Japan, to allow the country's insurance industry to rebuild itself and take part in international business.

'It was Geoffrey Hudson who influenced the Americans to drop their opposition to the idea of tariffs,' says Robin Snook, formerly of the Mercantile & General, who knew Japan well. 'He was hailed by the Japanese as the saviour of their insurance industry.' One of the key events that followed was the restructuring of the pre-war Toa Re, of which Mr Hashimoto now became Chief Executive.

Thus Hudson held the key to many valuable contacts in the Japanese world. 'Hudson was a man of enormous vision,' Dieter Losse sums up. 'He had a great affection for the Japanese and a strong understanding of their culture. There was also a strong chemistry between him and ourselves.' When the time came for Hudson to retire, he worked first as Eastern Manager for the Mercantile & General before being engaged by John Merison and Dieter Losse as Greigs' Tokyo adviser.

For a small and, from the Japanese point of view, relatively unknown company, Greigs had been highly successful in making its presence known. But one area of business still remained closed: the huge Japanese earthquake reinsurance account, including the city of Tokyo itself, in the notoriously high-risk 'zone five'. A newcomer to this business would have to prove itself in what, in reinsurance terms, was the really big league. Recalls Dieter Losse: 'We thought long and hard before we made a play for the lead on the earthquake business, and we held off till we felt we were ready for it. What was important was that we had the credibility and infrastructure. Would we have the systems and finance in place to cope with a very large claim?'

The element of caution was to be justified by events. Fond as the Japanese were of 'Hurricane John', as Merison was known in Tokyo, continuity was an important consideration in the Japanese business philosophy. Seiji Yamada, formerly a Managing Director of the Toa Re, now Greigs' senior representative in Tokyo, recalls that 'Mr Hashimoto took the decision when John Merison first went to see him that he would give him two or three years to see how persistent he was.'

Meanwhile the answer to Dieter Losse's question, when it came, would take Greigs to the top of the reinsurance world class.

CHAPTER SIX

Two and two make five

Regis House, home of the newly merged company Greig Fester

Towards the end of the 1960s it was becoming clear to John Greig and his colleagues that the company was in need of a rethink. Greigs had had a great deal of luck over forty years: in the talents and personality of Walter Greig himself, in such happy episodes as that of the sergeant-cook and in the inventiveness that had brought so many ideas to the London market over the previous ten years. Now, however, it was time for a change. As Dieter Losse says, 'In those days Greigs' reputation was much greater than its business. John Greig realised that it had to change – and that transformed it.'

What John Greig was seeking in particular was a new approach. 'For many years,' he says, 'the accounting and administration of the firm had been successfully run by Douglas Rathbone on the back of an envelope. The time had come when we needed to adopt modern management and accounting techniques to cope with the company's next phase of expansion.'

His feelings were not only on behalf of Greigs but also of the London market as a whole, for this was the period when the UK companies were beginning to be aware of their loss of influence worldwide, and when the brokers were going to the ends of the earth to bring back the reinsurance business which was being seen as London's new strength. 'Greigs had an important part to play in this,' he says, 'because we were one of the very few specialist reinsurance brokers. But as late as 1970 we only had a shoestring staff.'

His first move was to appoint a firm of management consultants to suggest ways in which the company might be run more effectively. Their findings confirmed what he already knew: that costs had been rising faster than commission income, that the organisation structure was inadequate as Greigs moved from being a small to a medium-sized business, and that administrative and clerical procedures needed to be rationalised if they were to provide the better service that was needed. The consultants applauded the broking side's rapid growth – but agreed with John Greig's own view that 'the present organisation is confused and needs to be reviewed and improved if the company is to expand in a controlled and profitable manner'.

The report did not explore one other idea that had been maturing in the minds of John Greig and John Merison – who with Douglas Rathbone made up the triumvirate that was now running Greigs. The new idea was that the client base might be broadened if they were to use the accumulated cash reserves to buy another broking house. John Greig's thoughts were by now moving in other ways as well. One idea that was completely novel at the time was for seminars, when senior management and staff might plan the strategic objectives of the company. A happy coincidence came when he attended a business management course at the Oxford Centre for Management Studies – later Templeton College – where Desmond Graves, one of the Fellows, happened to have been a friend of many years' standing. Later, he was to play an important consulting role for over twenty years, particularly in helping to organise the seminars at which he assumed the role of devil's advocate to help stimulate provocative discussion.

Comparative budgets as estimated in the pre-merger talks.

	Greigs 1974 Budget	Festers 1974 Estd
Proportional	262,000	370,000
Non-proportional	410,000	185,000
Facultative	24,000	12,000
Aviation	68,000	1,000
Marine	84,000	15,000
TOTAL	848,000	583,000

The more John Greig and John Merison thought about it, the more a merger began to look like a possible route Greigs might take – but a merger with whom? The obvious choice would be another reinsurance broker, ideally one with a very different and therefore complementary client base. And it so happened that one winter's day in 1972, John Merison found himself talking to Duncan Allen of Festers on the touchline of a Kent prep school where both their boys went. Gradually talk of a possible merger came up.

There were several ways in which Greigs and Festers looked like ideal partners. Festers had historic connections in Europe, while Greigs was strongest in Latin America and the countries of the Commonwealth. Greigs, it was true, was beginning to find new strengths in Japan – but with very different companies from those with whom Festers' links went back a long time. Apart from their specialist areas, the two companies had tantalising differences in style: Desmond Graves, in a comprehensive analysis of the eventual merger from its first to last stage, characterises Festers personnel as 'methodical administrators who above all like to get the system right ... good at cutting out bad risks but not so good at putting on the good risks.' Those at Greigs, on the other hand, were 'people who like to take risks and get a good feeling when they're doing something exciting.' Says Bill Hill, a Greig Fester director who has worked in both firms:

> *Greigs has always been go-ahead, thrusting, wanting to get business and worrying afterwards what they were going to do with it. Festers always pre-planned, with staff in place before they took on business ... they wouldn't take it on unless they knew they were adequately staffed. At Greigs it was the other way round. When you got snowed under, you suddenly got staff.*

The touchline meeting had sparked a process which was to go on glowing over the next two years like a slow fuse – though this is not to say there were not moments when the slow fuse might have spluttered. Michael Simmonds, who came in on the financial side in 1973, recalls that during the later 1960s the accounting at Greigs had received a good deal less attention than the broking. 'The reinsurance ledgers had not been reconciled with the company's accounts,' he says:

> *It was a serious enough problem for the Festers people not to want to pursue the merger, because they had been advised not to by their accountant. Duncan Allen, in particular, didn't want to go ahead. It was Brian Wallas who took up a positive position and said they could overcome that: he was strongly in favour because of the complementary business that the two companies had. Festers were strong in Europe and Greigs were strong elsewhere.*

Looking back, it would seem that there was a great deal to be said for the merger to proceed at a relatively slow pace, while John Greig, its mastermind, insisted on having all procedures properly thought out. Says Desmond Graves:

Michael Simmonds

He was very keen on holding the companies together, that they must proceed with caution. All too often a merger is something that happens from two managements meeting in smoke-filled rooms, with each side defending its own corner. This was the opposite, because John Greig sought people's views. His idea was that there should be no immediate redundancies, that where possible nobody should get hurt.

Adds John Greig himself:

My main wish was to get the best from everyone and the best from each company. We weren't merging because we thought we wouldn't survive if we didn't merge, but because we thought we would do better. We saw they had strengths we didn't have, and the other way round. Together we were stronger than we were as separate companies. Two and two made five.

In a later interview he added another word on the problems of holding a group of highly individual and often difficult people together. 'I think the sort of people that I need here work better in a consensus-style atmosphere because they have to be capable of strong independent action and I really need to be somebody who holds them together rather than telling them precisely what to do – my job is to make the organisation cohere.'

Talks between the two brokers and their merchant banks – Greigs was represented by Barings, with whom there had been links since Walter's Buenos Aires days – went on for over two years. Then, on 30 April 1974, three months after Festers' centenary and three years after Greigs' jubilee, the merger was announced to an amazed staff, none of whom had the slightest idea it was being discussed. At 9 a.m. on the morning of 1 May, telephonists who had always answered with the names of 'Greigs' or 'Festers' suddenly heard themselves announcing 'Greig Fester' for the first time.

On the personal and human side, John Greig's consideration for his staff – and Brian Wallas's for Festers – had been the strongest influence on the whole sequence of events. Recalls Desmond Graves: 'When the merger took place there were two chief accountants. Normally when that happens in a merger, the tougher one stays. In Greigs' case, they both stayed for a long time.' And Bill Hill, who had been on Greigs' staff and then gone to Festers in the late 1960s because his prospects looked better there, remembers hoping there would be no embarrassment in coming back: 'John Merison came over and said "You're all right, aren't you, Bill?" It was typical both of his kindness and the way the merger was done. He was making sure I knew I was welcome, coming back to the old firm.'

Meanwhile the days of the founding Greig brothers were gradually fading. 'To the ends of their lives, all three of them were very close,' recalls Jean Murphy, daughter of Kenneth, eldest of the brothers, who died in 1960. Leonard Greig lived to the age of 85. 'Right to the last he kept up a terrific interest in the firm,' remembers his daughter Audrey. 'He would still go to the office two days a week, saying he thought he ought to keep an eye on things.'

Walter Greig did not live quite long enough to see the merger take place, although he knew and was pleased about it. Through the early 1970s he had been coming up to London from Walton Heath: sitting in his office with the door always open, he would chat to old and new friends. Even at 87 he was full of enthusiasm and zest for life. 'He was intrigued by everything,' says his daughter Elspeth, 'and he never believed bad of anyone. He bought pictures, he took an interest in books, sports, languages, and ancient buildings. He would read Scott and Trollope – always the classics – and walk all over Walton Heath in his eighties.'

Suitably for the partners in so happy a marriage, Mildred and Walter Greig were not divided in death. Mildred died in the spring of 1973 and Elspeth arranged for her father to be looked after by an old friend. 'Three weeks after my mother died,' she recalls,

> *I rang up as usual and he told me he had arranged for Bob the chauffeur to take him the next day to the office. He asked, as he always did, about his grandchildren, but I felt there was something strange about him. Early next morning his doctor, who was a young woman, rang, and I told her I was pleased to hear from her because I'd been worried. She said 'You don't need to worry any more'. He had died quietly in the night, probably from a stroke.*

'To the day of his death, his presence was an inspiration to those who worked around him,' John Greig told a staff meeting held after his father's death, speaking too of his integrity, his energy and

Two and two make five

continual willingness to tackle something new, taking the example of his reaction to the Perón regime's threat to nationalise reinsurance. 'How can we turn this to our advantage?' Walter Greig had asked, and one senses something almost Elizabethan about the zestful, joyous way in which his mind worked. Yet deeper still was the strength of family affection, at its most endearing in his sense of exile in Argentina while his brothers were at the Western Front in the 1914 war. 'I remember my mother telling me that Uncle Walter in one of his letters home said he would start a business so the boys would have something to come back to after the war,' his niece Meryl wrote recently to John Greig. Perhaps it is not fanciful to suggest that the quality and integrity for which Greig Fester is famed today stemmed not only from the desire to make money but also from his human warmth.

Greigs had become a Lloyd's broker in 1963, at the beginning of a time when prospects for the world's insurance markets were looking good.

Hurricane Betsy hits Miami in 1965. Greigs' connections with the USA were slight so the firm was unaffected by the hurricane.

Even before the dramatic rise of oil prices, not only inflation but also the sheer escalating size of everything from jet aircraft to supertankers meant that insurance premiums were showing dramatic increases, bringing new opportunities for reinsurers, while the overseas brokers were doing well from sterling's weakness.

For Lloyd's underwriters, the 1970s was a time of recovery from their worst-ever loss: Hurricane Betsy which, in 1965, had done millions of dollars' worth of damage as it had ripped up America's east coast, destroying homes and oil-rigs. The £38 million loss it had brought to Lloyd's was, it was said, the result of optimistic underwriting: many syndicates had been happy to accept the reinsurance of great American companies while failing to realise just how large was their exposure, and one of the results of Betsy was that Lloyd's now recognised the need to put its underwriting house in order.

Greigs, who had only slight connections with the USA, was not affected by Betsy – but its turn would come next. It came, to be precise, on Christmas Eve 1974, when Cyclone Tracy hit the Australian city of Darwin, where 40,000 people had to be evacuated – 600 of them packed into a single jumbo jet – from the city centre whose water and power supplies had been cut. Deputy Premier Jim Cairns, standing in for Gough Whitlam who was on a Christmas world tour, visited the city, commenting that it looked as if it had been hit by an atom bomb. The official casualty lists reported forty-five dead, with nine out of every ten houses destroyed. The Australian insurance companies, many of them long-standing Greigs clients, were facing huge claims.

Almost as much as Hurricane Betsy, Tracy was to affect reinsurance markets worldwide, for their enthusiasm for the any one risk covers had led reinsurers to ignore the possibility that a single event might one day lead to a catastrophe destroying

Darwin after Cyclone Tracy, 1974. This event proved to be the baptism of fire for the newly merged company, which gained in status by its major involvement in the aftermath.

buildings on such a huge scale. Probably no other city in the world, analysts assessed, had buildings of such flimsy construction, of such high values and with such a high percentage of insurance against damage caused by windstorm.

Most Greig Fester staff had seen the disaster on the TV news on Christmas Day: the claims department management returned one day early from the Christmas holiday, wondering where it was going to start to count the cost. What was clear to everyone was that Greig Fester, a small company with an unusually large Australian portfolio, would have the eyes of the insurance world upon it.

Normally, reinsurance brokers wait until claims come in before they start looking for payment from the reinsurer. Such a procedure might take several weeks or months. It was clear in this instance that a disaster on the Darwin scale needed more imaginative action – while a rapid response from Greig Fester would help to establish the company as a top name in world reinsurance. When Claims Manager Geoffrey Hall reached the office from his home at Southend-on-Sea, he began contacting all the worldwide companies who had reinsured the Australian companies. 'Often,' he recalls, 'we could only tell them what they knew from the newspapers, that there had been a major loss. We recommended they should expect to have to pay up on the first and second layers, possibly also the third and fourth layers.'

At the same time he and his colleagues, Linda Curson and Steve Waters, began making a list of the London companies involved: there were 200 of them, and a hundred Lloyd's syndicates, and, because the reinsurance practice requires proof of loss, each would have to be called on and agreement obtained. 'We found an old suitcase in the office,' explains Geoffrey Hall, 'which we stuffed with evidence of the disaster in the form of newspaper cuttings, telexes and photos. We made our appointments with each company at quarter-of-an-hour intervals, told them we'd do our best to be there on time, but that we might be up to two hours late.'

At the Australian end, because of the Christmas break, it took a few days for the Darwin news to sink in. John Allison, widely known to his friends as the expert of Australian reinsurance, had been spending Christmas in England. Returning to Sydney on Boxing Day when he heard the Darwin news, he phoned Greg Hoorda, a relatively new member of his staff, who had come to the accounts department six months before from banking. 'He told me to get off my backside and that I wasn't on holiday any more,' grins Greg Hoorda, who had been with friends in Canberra for Christmas. 'He just said "you're a banker, we need to control this".'

During the first week in January, John Allison was on his way back to London again – this time to report progress to a meeting of underwriters in Greig Fester's Lime Street office. He was able to bring them estimates of the likely cost: average property values in Darwin were $27,000 and around 9,000 properties had been hit.

Over the next few weeks the work was fast and furious for seven days a week, in both the office and at Hoorda's house in Sydney:

> *We set up a bank account on a separate basis so it was nothing to do with the ordinary Greig Fester business. Each reinsurer had one cashbook for each cover. The whole principle was to keep it simple ... I always remember the first payment we received. It was at the end of the first week, from the British and European in London, for a million dollars. The local bank manager couldn't believe it – I don't think he'd ever seen a million dollars coming in one transaction.*

By now Darwin itself had been evacuated, so that individual policyholders were having to go to insurance company offices all over Australia to claim.

At the same time the London team were obtaining block settlements from the London reinsurers which streamlined the normal cumbersome collection procedures. Because the claim had to be paid in Australian dollars which Lloyd's did not normally handle, Geoffrey Hall had to obtain authority from the Bank of England to deal in the money markets. 'We were making daily phone calls to the dealers to find out the best prices of the day,' he recalls. 'We had $9 million on the way to Australia within ten days.'

By now the whole question of the Darwin claims had become so large that Lloyd's themselves set up a committee chaired by Colin Murray, underwriter of the Kiln Syndicate. This committee, together with company reinsurers, appointed Robert Cole of Toplis and Harding to visit the Australian companies to see that the claims were being paid properly and promptly. Robert Cole, working on behalf of reinsurers together with Greig Fester, established a superb claims service in Sydney. It was so efficient that an insurance company in Australia would pay a claim in the morning and collect from reinsurers in the same afternoon.

Greg Hoorda remembers that the initial process of setting the office machinery going was a 24-hours-a-day job:

But once that was set up it was pretty smooth sailing. I think it went on for eighteen months before we closed it all up. But nobody had imagined the size of the claims. Two hundred million dollars might seem like chicken feed now, but not in those days. There was one reinsurer that got a premium of I think it was $560 for the twelve-month period and their claim was one and a quarter million. Of the roughly two hundred million paid out, approximately half came through Greigs' books.

The Darwin experience was incidentally good for Greig Fester in two ways. It was the first time the company had been seen as a major broker – particularly when larger rivals such as Sedgwick were following the Greig Fester example in finding a rapid, commonsense means to pay claims fast. The other good news about the Darwin experience was that it came so soon after the merger. 'There was a sense of unity resulting from what the two teams had now achieved together,' says John Greig. 'This made a dramatic difference to the new firm.'

The other immediate consequence of Darwin was that from then on the reinsurance underwriters would want far more information before taking on risks. Colin Murray recalls how the underwriters began to standardise the information they got from their clients. 'We decided we needed much more information than we had before,' he says:

We required in Australia, for instance, disclosure of the total insurance in force, split between dwellings and commercial and industrial buildings in bands up the east coast, so we had a whole lot of zones, and we could compare the exposure of our different clients. We could see what rates they should pay, how much cover they needed and how much they should carry themselves. By types of risk in specialised geographical areas, we got aggregate exposures.

Meanwhile, across the waters of the western Pacific, Greigs' long siege of the Japanese market had begun to pay off. John Merison's first reward for patience, Seiji Yamada, formerly a Managing Director of the Toa Re, believes, came three years after his first visit in the form of a reciprocal exchange – with the great prize coming in the early 1970s when the Toa Re appointed Greigs as principal broker for their huge new catastrophe reinsurance programme. This was an enormous break-through and the consequence of the deal, as we shall see, would be incalculable for Greig Fester.

In every sense the late 1970s and 1980s was a time of great expansion for the newly merged firm. Greig Fester had been steadily becoming a different kind of organisation from what it had been in the past, and in 1983 there came a restructuring which would stress the importance of the client rather than the product, with one person or one team being

Growth of Greig Fester Group, showing Profit, Commission and Shareholders' funds.

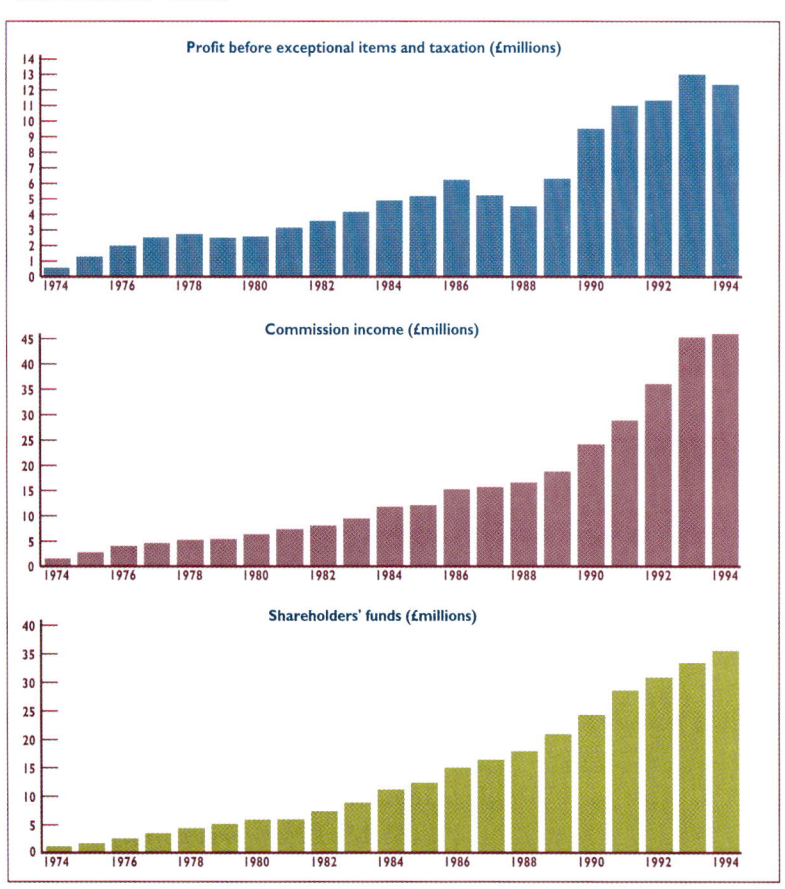

responsible for each client's business. At the same time staff numbers were rising rapidly – from 160 in 1975 to 250 in 1982 – while profits began to increase dramatically. In 1970, the year when John Greig had first approached the management consultants, brokerage had been £700,000. By 1974, the merger year, it had risen to £1.4 million. When Sedgwick, the London market's biggest broker, made an unsuccessful approach to take over the newly merged firm in 1982, this figure had risen five-fold to £7.788 million, and by 1990 brokerage was exceeding £20 million for the first time.

Expansion overseas was another new theme. In the past, Greigs' presence overseas had been limited to one or two key offices. In those days, says Dieter Losse, 'we always believed we could handle our business most efficiently from London and one or two carefully chosen locations, and that it was more efficient to send our travellers out to bring the business back.' Thus the Greigs banner overseas had notably been carried by the Australian office which had played such a key role over the Darwin claims. The story of the only other long-established office overseas, the one in South Africa, had begun in 1961. Its founder, John Kristeller, had been born in Königsberg and had escaped from Nazi Germany under the eyes of the SS. He had settled in South Africa and, having done a favour for Sentrakas, the South African farmers' co-operative insurer, had been offered their reinsurance as a return. Travelling to Europe to seek the help of larger companies, he happened to meet John Greig at Zurich airport and had explained the purpose of his visit. 'Don't do anything without talking to us,' John Greig told him, and within weeks the setting-up of W.T. Greig (South Africa) was the result.

The network of worldwide offices has grown notably in the last fifteen years. 'Since the mid-1980s,' Dieter Losse notes,

> *there has been a clear perception that we need to be much closer to a larger number of key markets. We have now established subsidiaries in the US – with offices in Auckland, Madrid, Mexico, Tokyo and Singapore. One particularly notable new departure was our acquisition of the MBM Re in France – the only reinsurance broking acquisition the group has made since the 1974 merger. This was a move to give ourselves a foothold in Europe with a company that could be integrated into the group but had a clear continental identity of its own. What all this adds up to is that we*

have come to realise that sitting in London, simply being a London broker, is not making us the sort of international company we want to be.

One very successful example of the role of the overseas office, he explains, is the one in Japan which is basically designed to supplement the main service from London:

London still plans and services the business but with the active support of an organisation that is thoroughly Japanese. From a modest beginning with Mr Yamada and one talented university graduate, we have built up an office with a small but highly trained Japanese staff. Looking ahead, we expect this office to grow in importance and to take over more and more of the role played by London. And this, we hope, will be a model for other markets.

Greig Fester was now growing in stature and reputation every year, and 1986 brought a recognition that was both public and personal when John Greig was elected to the Council of Lloyd's. His election came at a time of great significance in the history of the market, which had been dogged by problems and scandals. In the same year, the Queen had opened the prestigious new building which many people hoped might bring a clean start.

Meanwhile John Greig himself had made a generous response to the report of Sir Patrick Neill's committee on the Lloyd's market which had been published in the New Year. One of Neill's recommendations was that the effective control of the market by insiders should come to an end: with this in view, the proposal was that the number of working members of the Council should be reduced from sixteen to twelve, leaving a majority of places for non-working names or people co-opted from outside Lloyd's. John Greig's immediate and characteristic reaction was an offer to resign, thus leaving a vacancy for an outsider to fill. His gesture was suitably rewarded eighteen months later when, standing for the Council again, he was returned with the highest majority of any candidate. In 1991 he was elected one of the two Deputy Chairmen, continuing in this post for two years.

Given the responsibility for training and the regulation of brokers in addition to the day-to-day handling of Lloyd's affairs, he played a

Two and Two Make Five

The Council of Lloyd's in 1991. John Greig, Deputy Chairman, is second from right, front row.

significant role during a time of recurring crisis for the market. 'I felt it was right to spend time serving the community of which we are a part, and to help in supporting our most important market,' is how he sums up what must have been a heavily demanding two years.

The market which he had done so much to support was by now facing increasing problems. Following the huge losses on American liabilities, the last years of the decade brought a series of natural disasters so formidable as to make it seem that the elements themselves had declared war on the reinsurers. The year 1987 was marked by the first hurricane to strike the British Isles for two centuries. Swinging in from northern France, it cut a swathe through the southern counties and East Anglia at a cost of £1.2 billion to the insurance market. The year 1989 brought Hurricane Hugo to the USA, costing insurers $4.5 billion, not to mention sleepless nights at the thought that a similar storm might one day travel up the east coast to Manhattan. Greig Fester was often collecting as much as 10 per cent on these disasters – in worldwide terms, a very high proportion of the loss. In January and February 1990 more European storms cost insurers a total of $7.5 billion, the largest loss yet, and by then the retrocession market, which reinsures the reinsurers, found itself facing such huge claims that many of its underwriters pulled out. Meanwhile, the market shivered at the prediction that a repeat of the 1906 San Francisco earthquake could cause a total economic loss of around $200 billion.

There were problems that faced the insurance market as a whole. The new technology, it was being said, would have little room for the historic way of doing business between a broker and an underwriter. As phoneline services grew, there was more and more talk of low-cost direct dealing between the insured and the insurer.

In the new century, it seemed possible, the broker might have to start looking for a new role.

CHAPTER SEVEN

Today's professionals

Aerial view of Devon House (left of centre), framed by St Katharine's Dock and the Thames.

Over the years Greigs have moved their offices several times but, like most brokers, seldom more than a few streets outside the immediate periphery of Lloyd's. In 1992, finding themselves outgrowing their office space in Regis House, on the north side of London Bridge, they began to cast around for something both original and in keeping with their own style. Their eventual choice was Devon House, a handsome new office block on the newly restored area of St Katharine's Dock, which looked out on one side to the river below Tower Bridge, and on the other to St Katharine's colourful and historic vessels. Another plus was that the whole of the second floor was one huge open-plan room which fitted with the company philosophy that no one worked behind partitions. The only minus was that it was some way from Lloyd's; this, it was decided, would be accommodated by running a half-hourly bus between St Katharine's Way and Lime Street. The move to Devon House, made on August Bank Holiday 1992, has continued to justify the comment by Peter Keats: 'If you want to attract the best people, give them the best workplace.'

Watercolour of Devon House by John Ross, commissioned by Greig Fester to mark the move to the new headquarters in August 1992.

One of the things this book has sought to show is that the patterns of reinsurance have changed in each succeeding decade. From the beginning of the 1990s they were to change still more decisively as the whole role of the reinsurance broker was called into question.

Today's Professionals

Dieter Losse, now Group Chief Executive, traces the point of departure back to the great storms of 1987 and 1990. As a result of these huge claims, he explains, reinsurance premiums and therefore brokers' commissions were going up:

This was a time when the insurance companies were going through a lot of stress and strain, and it was quite clear that we had to do more to justify our levels of earnings. If our clients were going to be comfortable we realised we had got to do a lot more than we had ever done in the past.

Thus was born the concept of added-value service to clients which was to lead Greig Fester, as we shall see, into some unexpected new paths.

'Before 1987,' points out Andrew Clarkson, Greig Fester Group Board Director, 'very few British companies bought much in the way of catastrophe excess of loss reinsurance. Then, after the storms of 1990, we came under huge pressure because reinsurance prices were going up in multiples. And the money they were having to spend was making the general managements take a very close look at how they could control it.'

Other factors, too, Andrew Clarkson says, were helping to stir things. 'The summer of 1986 was very dry, which led to subsidence claims which in turn caused a lot of problems. And because of the recession a lot of companies were hit by domestic mortgage insurance claims. Up to then, very little of this was covered by reinsurance.'

So as the domestic insurance companies began to count the cost, there came a far closer scrutiny of what they spent on reinsurance. Recalls Dieter Losse:

The first thing that happened when the cost of reinsurance rose was that the decisions about it rocketed to the top of organisations and the general managers and financial directors wanted to know why. So that required a much more articulate defence, first of the reinsurance mechanics, and second of the cost and the services that supported that cost. So that put a huge spur on us to do more.

One response to this challenge was a largely original idea as to how reinsurance underwriters could be given more information about the potential costs of floods and windstorms in the UK. A small Greig Fester team began relating the number of houses covered by client companies to their postcodes, then to the actual total value of the houses. Soon they were able to start displaying complex information on electronic maps. Next came the idea of a computer model that would simulate the effect of floods and storms across the UK.

A reserve of information was built which, only a short time before, would have been seen as remote from reinsurance. The Post Office helped with details of the location of housing stock. The Buildings Research Establishment explained about the variations between Scotland and the south-east of England when it comes to how far a building will withstand wind-gusts. Touring various university departments of oceanography and earth sciences, the team learnt how floods are generated when low pressure over the North Sea is driven south, creating a bulge of the sea surface at the time of spring tides. 'By 1992,' project leader Andrew Mitchell says, 'we could show our clients the amount of exposure for specified postcodes as illustrations on a map.'

When Greig Fester moved into Devon House in the autumn of 1992, the team was reaching out into new fields: by now they were thinking in terms of a three-dimensional computerised map with an accuracy of at best plus or minus fifty centimetres in order to show the effect of varying degrees of flooding on an insurance company's portfolio. Encouraged by the Ordnance Survey, Greig Fester went ahead with the building of the first computerised map of the UK to predict the effects of floods with such extreme accuracy. With its help, the model can show the effect of a once-in-250-year flood as it affects any single house in the UK.

Greig Fester's first report on the Geographic Analysis Project – GAP – was published in 1993. Its stated aim was to assist clients in the management of their UK property business with regard to catastrophe exposures. Since then, the methods developed in the project have been adapted to meet the needs of worldwide clients exposed to catastrophes of all kinds.

GAP is one of several initiatives that look towards the future when, says David Spiller, Chief Executive of Greig Fester International Ltd, 'the broker's placement role will clearly become less important. The successful broker will require a deeper understanding of the financial implications of reinsurance. It will be

TODAY'S PROFESSIONALS

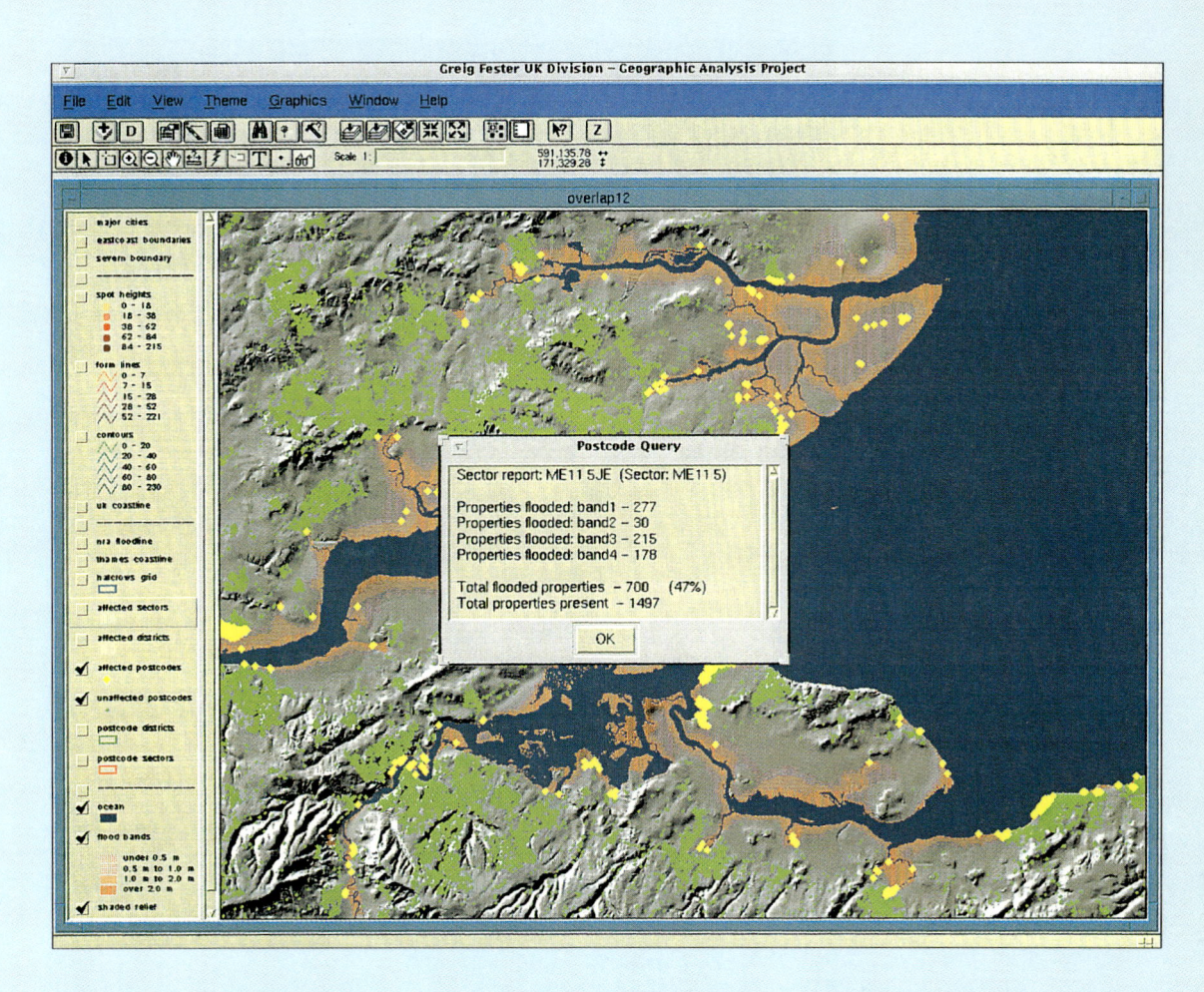

The Geographic Analysis Project has created a 3-D computer modelling program which simulates the effects on property of floods and storms. The program uses postcode data to produce a graphic representation of the way in which extreme weather conditions will impact upon any specified area.

The photograph of the Thames Estuary (above) shows a screenshot of the modelling process running on a Sun workstation which uses 16 gigabytes of memory. Each dot represents a postcode sector (on average 14 houses). The yellow areas indicate the properties which would be flooded on this simulation. The properties indicated by green dots are, as yet, unaffected. There is flooding inland along the banks of the rivers Swale, Crouch and Thames up to Stanford le Hope. Herne Bay, on the extreme right, where John Andrew Greig and his children were photographed circa 1897 (see p 11), would in places be under 2 metres of water.

Management seminar at Lainston House in 1989. Seminars have played an important and innovative role within the company since the late 1960s.

increasingly his function to advise clients on the nature and structure of their reinsurance programmes as part of the overall financial armoury an insurance company has to protect its balance sheet.'

Increasingly, throughout the Group, contact is with senior management and finance directors as reinsurance is often the second biggest item of expenditure for an insurance company after its wages bill. And the broker is expected to provide far more in the way of reports and advice than was the case a few years ago. 'Take, for example, a Danish client for whom we place the main reinsurance for their windstorm or their marine exposures. They will want a quarterly report on the state of the market. Are rates going up or down? Instead of excess of loss should they look at the possibilities of a stop-loss cover? What is the capacity situation?'

Dieter Losse takes the concept of service to clients several steps further:

The management of an insurance company has to manage not just the reinsurance risk but a whole range of other risks: its capital base, its investment portfolio, its currency risk, and its insurance exposures. We are now having to look at reinsurance as just one of the tools which an insurance company's senior executives can use in order to manage the variety of risks to which the business is prone. What we're now trying to give some coherence to, is how these risks are interdependent. How an

Today's Professionals

Smoke over Sydney as bushfires approach the outskirts of the city in January 1994.

insurance company's capital base develops, which means partly how the financial markets move, has a very direct influence on its reinsurance. The extent to which it may be exposed to a sudden change in value of major currencies will also influence the nature and extent of reinsurance it may buy. All this means we are beginning to look at reinsurance in a much broader context.

When Walter Greig began his company in 1921, it was a tale of two cities, London and Buenos Aires. Today, three-quarters of a century on, there is hardly a world capital or business centre where the name of Greig Fester is not known. Japan, first visited by Festers over eighty years ago, remains a cornerstone. Risks reinsured are not only those in the predominant area of earthquake and typhoon, but also covers for multinational companies as they move outside Japan, along with, for example, £450 million worth of shipowners' liability insurance covering the passengers on the ferryboats that ply between the islands.

Walter Greig would still find plenty of business flowing from the countries he visited: important earnings still come from South America, while in New Zealand there are few companies in the whole country that are not clients of Greig Fester. In Australia, Managing

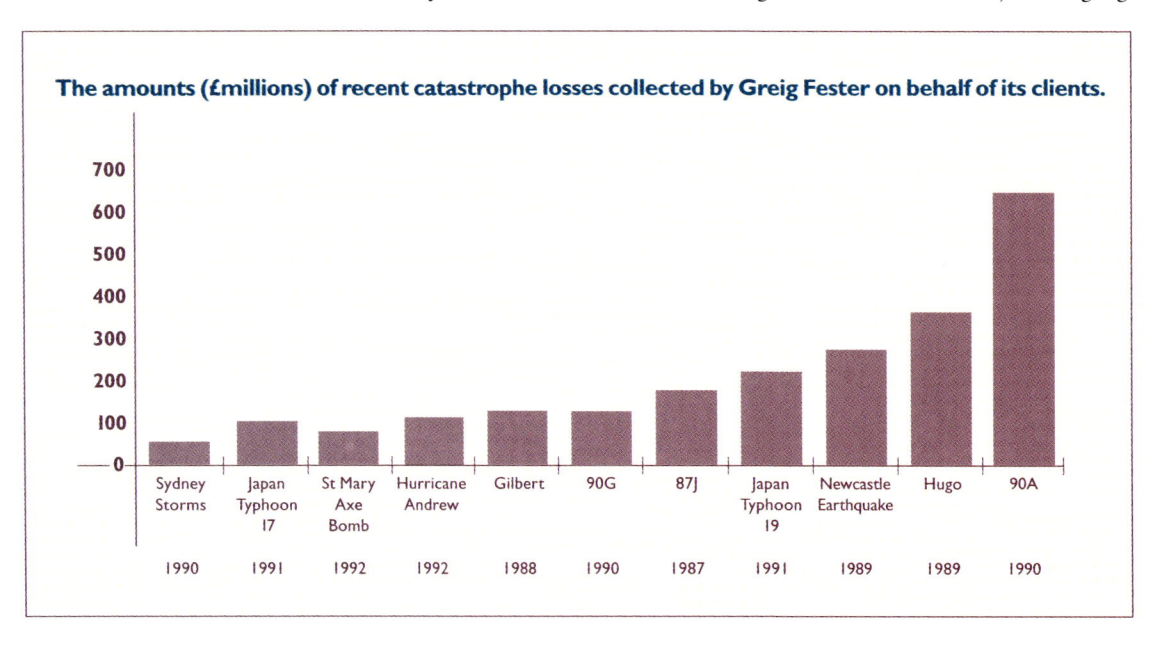

The amounts (£millions) of recent catastrophe losses collected by Greig Fester on behalf of its clients.

Sydney Storms	1990	~50
Japan Typhoon 17	1991	~100
St Mary Axe Bomb	1992	~75
Hurricane Andrew	1992	~110
Gilbert	1988	~130
90G	1990	~130
87J	1987	~180
Japan Typhoon 19	1991	~220
Newcastle Earthquake	1989	~270
Hugo	1989	~360
90A	1990	~650

Director Ray Carless has put research literally on the map with pioneering studies of earthquake and windstorms. Collaborating with the insurance companies as sponsors, Greig Fester has set up a research programme in which university academics research earthquake and windstorm potential in exposed territories. 'The thinking behind the research is that, in the past, insurance companies have bought reinsurance based on the mpl [maximum probable loss] they could suffer from a storm or earthquake or bushfire,' explains Ray Carless. 'What the new research has done is to drive that forward to give some much harder real-life facts.'

China is one of the countries with the most dramatic potential for reinsurance. 'Now they are trading with the rest of the world,' David Spiller says, 'their currency will become convertible and the possibilities since the deregulation of the market are enormous. There are significant natural-perils exposures and, in the new economic climate, both the state-owned and newly formed private companies will need reinsurance protection.'

Europe is moving into the foreground for Greig Fester, following the establishment of representation in France and Spain, while in Germany, historically the company has always been close to the major reinsurers. One of the incidentally agreeable features of Greig Fester is its tendency – perhaps flowing from Walter's Latin American affection – to employ staff who have an affinity with the countries they deal with. David Spiller, for instance, has close links with the Scandinavian countries which form part of the territories with which he is concerned: descended from a family with close Norwegian links, he spent his early working life in Oslo and his wife is a Norwegian doctor.

Almost certainly the future will see a greater development of brokers' teamwork and a more intense professionalism. 'Over the last four or five years,' says Dieter Losse,

> *we have already begun to see a qualitative change, both in our commitment to teamwork and in terms of the type of people we're recruiting. These are not just graduates but bright and innovative graduates. We are in the process of becoming a much more professional firm, much less hierarchical: a series of professionals who look after clients in groups.*

Crucially, he believes, there are perhaps three elements which distinguish Greig Fester from its competitors and will help the company to succeed even though the role of the broker is being challenged and transformed. 'In the first place,' he points out,

we have over the years been fortunate in being able to build up the financial resources of the company. The management today has the benefit of substantial capital which gives our clients confidence in the long-term continuity of our service and allows us to avoid short-termism and instead take decisions which enhance the value of the business over time ... The second point is that since the early days of Walter Greig there has been a readiness on the part of the shareholders to allow the senior executives and staff to participate in the equity of the company in a meaningful way. Over the decades this has enabled us to attract and retain dedicated staff which has given us cohesion. Finally, there is a commitment to provide independent advice which is valued by our clients for its objectivity.

From Nicholas Lane to Devon House: in just under three-quarters of a century, Greigs has travelled not much more than half a mile from the spot where Walter Greig and his brothers unloaded their 1920s' taxi-cab. Over the same time the company has been transformed from a not too arduous three-man office to a vast and influential international business.

In terms of leadership there has been contrast, too. For just as Greig Fester owes its origins to Walter, it owes its continuance to his son, John, who saw what was needed to make it viable in a new age. For a final word I went to see him in his office overlooking Tower Bridge, close to the two Greig portraits depicting Walter, the happy extrovert, and John's own more questing, philosophic features. As we approach the new century, I asked, would there always be a need for brokers?

He thought there would, but that it would be greatly changed:

It's going to be a market of fewer but bigger players. A market where small companies will find it increasingly difficult to survive. When you have fewer and bigger entities, there won't be the same need for the broker going round wearing out shoe leather... but his experience will

JOHN S. GREIG

Greig Fester Group Board in the Regis House Boardroom, 1990 (left to right): Tim Abell, Peter Keats, Michael Simmonds, John Greig, Dieter Losse, Brian Wallas and, Company Secretary, Frank Hitchman.

still be needed, because our business requires a marketplace to absorb the huge liabilities which will still require reinsurance. When there's a whole range of products available you need the experience of a broker to find a way through that marketplace. But I think the broker will also become involved with other elements of risk. He will be thinking of his clients' investment portfolio, his exchange problems – he will become more and more of a risk adviser.

Did that mean that reinsurance would itself change?

It has changed many times in the past, as your book shows. If we're crystal-gazing some years ahead, we can't ignore the possible development of the Catastrophe Futures Market. This is a sophisticated concept, but what basically happens is that the company buys the right to receive an amount of money depending on the catastrophe loss experience in a given geographical area. For instance, take the west coast of the USA: if the general loss experience in that area exceeds a certain figure, then the company makes a recovery. I can imagine that particularly if we have another series of catastrophes, and if the capacity in the conventional market falls away, then this could become something people would be very interested in and, if this proves to be the case, then we have to be at the forefront.

How much, I asked, might Greig Fester itself change over another twenty years, bearing in mind that the last twenty had seen the change from a small company to a much larger one?

Being a bit old-fashioned, I would prefer to go on more or less as we are in terms of the sort of company that we seek to be. There is still plenty of scope for us to expand both in areas of the world where we are not so strong at the moment and in other classes of reinsurance business. But the real basis of our success is an ability to attract the absolutely top-rate people by offering a structure which encourages teams to come together and take on the challenges the market has to offer. With people of that quality, you've got to leave them on a fairly loose rein. You've got to allow them to have their heads while imposing the overall direction of the company. Take the GAP concept, something we've all been proud of being first in the field with. If we had had a different structure, if for instance we were a public company, we might have found it more difficult to invest considerable sums in something which is a long-term venture by a dedicated and very motivated team.

If your father were here today, I asked, how much of the company would he recognise?

I like to think it's still run according to his precepts. Service to clients, innovative ideas, thinking ahead, enthusiasm, running a company with good people and giving them their heads. Ethical principles and standards: our philosophy is very much the same as it was in his time. There's always room for people in this business to be creative, and this is one of the great joys. It's unlike the Stock Exchange where the product you're selling has a predetermined shape: in reinsurance you go in with a blank sheet. You have the intellectual challenge of working out with the reinsured a way of doing business, a product which satisfies both sides. So you've actually got to create a new product time and time again rather than deal in a product that's already there. That's why I can think of few other places where I would have had more satisfaction and more challenge than being a reinsurance broker.

Kobe, Japan, is struck by a huge earthquake on 17 January 1995.

Today's Professionals

In the end, I thought, as I left the fourth floor of Devon House, what matters is the fascination of the business. Passing the library door I noticed there was something missing – the wallmap of the world with its fringe of fire that marks the earthquake zones. Later I found that on that particular January morning, it had been taken down – for the Japan Division to study in relation to the Kobe earthquake. From a stricken city in Japan to flooded homes in East Anglia, no other business mirrors world events so completely as reinsurance does.

In a less spectacular way, it is something the modern world could scarcely be without. Reinsurance might sometimes seem to concern only the higher reaches of finance – yet an excess of loss layer will as often relate to the insurance of ordinary factories and houses. It is reinsurance which pays the claims for small businesses and homeowners anywhere from Manchester to Melbourne.

But perhaps the most lasting impression is of a company concerned with principles as well as profits. 'I dread coming short of what is right,' wrote Walter Greig from Buenos Aires in 1914, and the message is one whose meaning in a world of shifting standards has continued. In the end what makes a company exceptional is the combination of such values with professional innovation: at Greig Fester, both have helped to create a company which, on the threshold of a new century, is likely to continue to play a vital role in the story of reinsurance.

Glossary of specialist terms

Aggregate exposures Information relating to a reinsured company's property portfolio normally required by reinsurers to assess the potential effect of a catastrophe loss occurring in a selected geographical area.

All-risks A term used to describe a policy covering fortuities generally, though not inevitabilities such as wear and tear or depreciation. It is sometimes loosely used to describe a policy that covers a number of specified risks, though not all.

Any one event A method of excess of loss reinsurance protection (*see* Excess of loss, below) under which the reinsurer reimburses the reinsured company for the 'excess loss' arising from the accumulation of losses involved in one catastrophe.

Any one risk A method of excess of loss reinsurance protection (*see* Excess of loss, below) under which the reinsurer reimburses the reinsured company for the 'excess loss' arising from a single risk.

Catastrophe Futures Market A market managed by the Chicago Board of Trade which enables insurers to hedge an insurance portfolio against future catastrophe losses.

Co-insurance Where a number of insurers each cover a proportion of a risk or where a policy requires the insured to bear a part of each loss.

Excess of loss A form of reinsurance that covers a reinsured company's losses only to the extent that they exceed a specified amount. It would normally stipulate a maximum sum payable by the reinsurer.

Facultative reinsurance The reinsurance of individual risks by offer and acceptance wherein the reinsurer retains the 'faculty' to accept or reject each risk offered.

Layer A term used to denote a stratum of cover on excess of loss reinsurance (*see* Excess of loss, above).

Line An amount of risk or liability equal to that which the reinsured company retains for its own account.

Proportional treaty A reinsurance agreement binding the reinsured company to cede and the reinsurer to accept a proportionate share of all risks ceded to the treaty.

Reciprocal reinsurance An exchange of proportional reinsurance treaties (*see* Proportional treaty, above) between two companies.

Stop-loss cover A form of reinsurance whereunder the reinsurer reimburses the reinsured company for a specified loss ratio or amount by which the latter's incurred losses during a calendar year for a specified class of business exceed a specified loss ratio or amount.

Syndicates Groups of underwriters on whose behalf insurances are accepted, each underwriter taking a proportion of the insurance for him/herself, without assuming liability for the proportions taken by the other members of the group.

Further reading

Francis, E.V., *London and Lancashire History: The History of the London and Lancashire Insurance Company Ltd* (Newman Neame, 1962)

Gibb, D.E.W., *Lloyd's of London: A Study in Individualism* (Macmillan & Co., 1957)

Golding, C.E., *A History of Reinsurance with Sidelights on Insurance* (Waterlow & Sons Ltd, 1st edition 1927)

Minnitt, J., *The Sun Life Story* (Sun Life, 1985)

Raynes, H.E., *A History of British Insurance* (Pitman & Sons Ltd, 2nd edition 1964)

Supple, Barry, *The Royal Exchange Assurance: A History of British Insurance 1720–1970* (Cambridge University Press, 1970)

Trebilcock, Clive, *Phoenix Assurance and the Development of British Insurance, vol. I 1782–1870* (Cambridge University Press, 1986)

Acknowledgements

Special thanks are due to the following for permission to reproduce photographs and illustrations:

La Buenos Aires Compañia de Seguros (*Visas e Historias de la Avenida de Mayo*), pp 5, 47; Guildhall Library, Corporation of London, p 6; Sun Life Assurance Society plc, p 12; *Hinterland* 158 (2/1993) (used by permission of editor), p 23; Mund & Fester, pp 27, 28, 54; Les Hunt, p 33; Topham Picture Library, pp 35, 41, 51, 56; National Maritime Museum, p 40; Royal Geographical Society, p 43; *The Adelaide Advertiser*, p 59; Guardian Assurance, p 60; Kümmerley & Frey, p 63; the Rathbone family, p 69; Land Securities Properties Ltd, p 79; Popperfoto, pp 85 (UPI), 108; NRSC (Airphoto Group), p 95; Stevens/Fairfax Photo Library, p 101.

All other pictures, documents and illustrations are provided courtesy of the Greig Fester archives.

Every effort has been made to obtain permission for the reproduction of the illustrations and photographs in this book; apologies are offered to anyone whom it has not been possible to contact.

The quote from *The Times* on p 65 is © Times Newspapers Limited, 1954.

Index

Abell, Tim, Greig Fester Group Board Director, *106*
Adelaide;
 earthquake (1954), 65
 damage, *59*, 65
Aequitas Re of Gothenburg (Sweden), client, Fester, Fothergill & Hartung, 64
airlines, passengers, Lloyd's policies (1926), 50–1
 insurance premiums increase, jet aircraft, 86
Allen, Duncan, Partner, Fester, Fothergill & Hartung, 72
 in merger talks, 81
 initially opposed merger, 82
Allison, John, Manager, W.T. Greig Ltd (Australia), 71
 organises Darwin relief for Greig Fester, 87–8
 reports on damage and cost, 88
Andrews, John, underwriter, W.T. Greig Ltd, formerly of Northern Assurance Company Limited, recollection of 1970s, 65
Antwerp, Mund & Fester office (1874), *27*, 28
Archer, family history, 8–9
Archer, John, of Leslie, Perthshire, married daughter of George Greig, 8
Archer, Thomas, minister, brother of John Archer, 8–9
Avenida de Mayo, Buenos Aires, *5*, *47*
 Royal Exchange Assurance branch office at, 15

Bannister, Jim, analyses London reinsurance market in 1960s, 60–1
Baring Brothers, merchant bankers, 17
 represent W.T. Greig Ltd at merger negotiations, 83
Bentley's codebook, for decoding cables, 50
British and European (London), payment, Darwin account, Cyclone Tracy, 88
British Insurance Group, Geoffrey Hudson's employer, Tokyo, 76
brokers, *see* reinsurance
Buenos Aires, *see* Avenida de Mayo; Calle 25 de Mayo; Conte Restaurant; Extranjeros Club; Walter T. Greig; Sir John Hawkshaw; R.W. Roberts; Royal Exchange Assurance Corporation
Buildings Research Establishment, assisted Geographic Analysis Project, 98
burglary insurance, Havana, Walter Greig reports on, 41

C.E. Golding & Co., reinsurance brokers, 73
C.E. Heath and Co. (London), Royal Exchange Buildings, 49
Cairns, Jim, Deputy Premier of Australia, 1974, visited Darwin devastated by Cyclone Tracy, 86
Calle 25 de Mayo, Buenos Aires, Walter Greig's office, 15
Carless, Ray, Managing Director, Greig Fester (Australia), pioneers earthquake and windstorm research, 102–3
Carlton Club, London, frequented by Greig brothers, 55
CAT87J, hurricane, southern England, 1987, *33*, *33*
 damage cost, 94
 cover for, 68, 97, *102*
 formative reinsurance catastrophe, 97, *102*
catastrophes;
 earthquake, Tokyo (1923), *56*
 plague, Argentine wheat harvest (1928), 49
 floods, UK, East Coast (1953), 68
 earthquake, Adelaide (1954), 64–65
 bushfires, Tasmanian (1959), 73
 Hurricane Betsy, USA, (1965), *85*, 86
 Cyclone Tracy, Darwin (1974), *86*, 86–9
 hurricane, CAT87J, UK (1987), *33*, *33*, 68, 94, 97, *102*
 Hurricane Hugo, USA, (1989), 94, *102*
 storms, Europe (1990), 94, 97, *102*
 bushfires, Australia (1994), *101*
 Kobe earthquake, Japan (1995), *108*, 109
 see also earthquakes; fire; flood; reinsurance; windstorms

Catastrophe Futures Market, possible reinsurance development, 106
Cazenove, Mr, reinsurance broker, Broad Street, 26
Changi prison, Singapore, Geoffrey Hudson imprisoned at, 76
Charing Cross (now Whitehall) Sun Life Assurance Office, 1912, *12*
Clarkson, Andrew, Greig Fester Group Board Director, promotes added-value service to clients, 97
Clunie, Margaret, Greig kinswoman, preserved Archer family Bible, 9
Clunie, Rebecca, mother of John Andrew Greig, 10
Cole, Robert of Toplis and Harding, Lloyd's appointee, Australia, Cyclone Tracy catastrophe, 88
with Greig Fester, establishes claims service, 88–9
Cologne Re, first German reinsurance company (1853), 25
Commercial of Australia, interviews Walter Greig, cover for malicious damage, 50
Commercial Union (London), client of Sun Fire Office, 13, 26
Compagnie des Propriétaires Réunis (Brussels), negotiated first European reinsurance treaty (1821), 25
Compagnie Royale (Paris), 24–5
construction exposures;
Havana (1926), 41
risk factors to private houses and businesses, 32–33, 97–8, 109
sawmill, 'classic hazard', 32, 33
rate for malicious damage, 50
homes destroyed, Hurricane Betsy, 86
property values, Darwin, Cyclone Tracy, 86–8
Australia, 89
subsidence claims, UK, 97
flood research, UK, 97–8, *99*
Conte Restaurant, Buenos Aires, *49*
cotton mill, Calcutta, hazard reinsured, 25
Council of Lloyd's (1991), *93*
Credito Italiano (Rome), 50
Criterion Restaurant (Victoria Hall), *13*
Cromer, Fester, Fothergill & Hartung evacuate to 1939, 57
Curson, Linda, Greig Fester Claims Officer, catastrophe relief facilitator, Darwin, Cyclone Tracy, 87
Cyclone Tracy (Darwin, Australia, 1974), 86, *86*
formative reinsurance catastrophe, 86

Greig Fester response, 87–9
damage and insurance costs, 88–9

Daniell, Ferrers, Fire Manager, Royal Exchange Assurance, Walter Greig letters to, 17, 18, 19
de Zaldo, Señor, La Metropolitana, Havana, greets Walter and Mildred Greig, 41
Devon House (London), Greig Fester's present head office, 95, 96, *96*, 98, 109
map of earthquake zones, 63, *63*
Diaz, José, La Metropolitana, Havana, greets Walter and Mildred Greig, 41
discusses reciprocal reinsurance, 53
Dowa (Japan), client, Fester, Fothergill & Hartung, 71
Dunedin (New Zealand), Walter and Mildred Greig visit, 42, 43, *43*, 45

Eagle Fire Company of New York, first recorded reinsurance treaty with Union Insurance Company (1813), 24
earthquakes;
'earthquake book' at Lloyd's, 63–4
Lloyd's premiums, 64
catastrophe reinsurance cover, 63–5, 68, 76, 102, *102*
formative reinsurance catastrophes, 65, *108*, 109
'earthquake countries', 74
'fringe of fire' world map, 63, *63*, 109
damage, 68
Tokyo (1923), *56*; 'zone five' risk, 76–7
Australia, research, 102
Adelaide (1954), 65
Kobe (1995), *108*, 109
Japan, risk, 102
Jamaica, risk, 64
San Francisco, risk, estimated cost, 94
see also catastrophes; reinsurance
Errol, Archibald, Director, Fester, Fothergill & Hartung;
wrote memoir regarding founding directors, 54
provides character of company, 55
comment on Fester's wartime evacuation, 57
Extranjeros Club, Buenos Aires, Walter Greig at, 17

Fabian Society, 72
Farmer, Harry, Director, Fester, Fothergill & Hartung;
'guiding spirit' of company, 55
portrait, *55*

'masterminds' post-war reciprocal trading, Japan, 71
promotes Brian Wallas and Duncan Allen, 72
died (1958), 72
Fester, Emil, son of Heinrich Fester, 54
Fester, Fothergill & Hartung (London);
early history, *26, 28, 30, 54–5, 54*
merger, 1909, 30, 54
premises;
No. 34 Nicholas Lane, 8, 26
Laurence Pountney Lane (1910), 8, 54
Rectory House, Southwark Bridge (1924), 55
character, of founders, 26–8, 54; of company, 55, 82
accredited, Lloyd's (1910), 54
international reinsurance contracts;
Europe, 57, 58, 71, 81
Jamaica, 64
Japan, 55, 71, 81–2
see also individual company entries
war-time evacuation, 57
World War II, detrimental effects, 57–8, 71
develops catastrophe reinsurance business, 64
post-war growth, 64, 71, 72–3
problems, takeover of client London & Lancashire, 72
empathy with W.T. Greig Ltd, 81–3
pre-merger budget estimates, 82
merger considerations, 82–3
Greig Fester founded (1974), 83
see also Duncan Allen; Archibald Errol; Harry Farmer; Bill Hill; W.T. Greig Ltd
Fester, Heinrich, co-founder Mund & Fester, Antwerp (1874), 28
portrait, *27*
Fester, Jules, brother of Heinrich, founder Mund & Fester, Hamburg (1876), 28
portrait, *27*
fire;
Christiania (now Oslo), Norway, ravaged (1858), 25
threat to business and private houses, 32
sawmill, classic hazard, 32–3
arson, fraudulent claims, 51
bomb, rates for threat, 50
risk, to sugar cane, 41
risks, ceded to IMAR (Argentina), 63
bushfire, annual aggregate bushfire clause, 68
losses, *102*; premiums, 103
Tasmania (1959), 73
Sydney (1994), *101*

First Bohemian Reinsurance Bank of Prague, early partnership with Fester, Fothergill & Hartung, 55
Fisher, B.B., Foreign Fire Manager, Royal Exchange Assurance, reports good news, reinsurance profits, 1932, 53
flood;
Australia (1954), insurance cover, 65
UK, East Coast (1953), 68
threat, UK East Coast, GAP, 97–8, *99*
Fothergill, Basil, son of Henry Fothergill, Partner, Mund & Fester, Liverpool, 30, 54
Fothergill, Henry, General Manager and 'guiding spirit', London & Lancashire Reinsurance Company, 30, 54

Galbraith, James, friend of Greig brothers and sergeant-cook, London Scottish territorials, 39
reinsurance associate, 43–4
General Strike (1926), effects of in London, 45
Geographic Analysis Project (GAP), Greig Fester innovation, catastrophe computer model of UK East Coast, 97–8, *99*
pride in, 107
Gibb, D.E.W., historian of Lloyd's, describes traditional practices, 14
Gill, Frank, Partner, Fothergill & Hartung;
joined company, 1958, 72
with Brian Wallas negotiated breakthrough contract with the Royal, 72–3
portrait, *72*
Golding, C.E., historian of reinsurance, describes historical backwardness of London market, 24
Grabscheid, Gustav, of Guardian Assurance, associate of Douglas Rathbone, champions 'any one risk' policies, 67
Graves, Desmond, Fellow, Templeton College, consultant to Greig Fester Ltd, 81
analyses merger proposals, 82–3
notes magnanimity of, 83
Great War, memories, 7
Greig family involvement, 7, 18–9, *18*, 22, 39, 85
disability of Leonard Greig, 7, 22, 38
death of Roy Greig, 7, 22
letters concerning, from Walter Greig, 18–9
cable concerning, from John Andrew Greig, 19
effects on insurance market, 25
Green, Lilias, née Greig, only daughter of John Andrew Greig, *11*
Greig, Admiral, family ancestor, Russian Navy, 8

Greig, Audrey, Leonard Greig's daughter, recalls father's loyalty to W.T. Greig Ltd, 84
Greig, Betsy, preserved Archer Bible, 9
Greig, David, tallow chandler, son of George Greig, 9
Greig, Eric, son of John Andrew Greig, died aged 7, 11
Greig family history, ancestry, 6–13, *11*, *12*
   occupations, 9–10
   insurance origins, 9–13
   wartime misfortune, 22
   marriages, Greig–Archer, 8
      Greig–Sibbald, 9
      Greig–Clunie, 10
      Greig–Thomson, 10
      Greig–Rowe, 38–9
Greig Fester Group;
   merger announcement (1974), 83
   premises;
      Lime Street (1974), 88
      Regis House (1974), *79*
      Devon House (1992), *95*, 96, *96*, 98, 109
   philosophy and organisation, 83, 85, 96–100, *100*, 102–4, *106*, 106–7, 109
   staff, efficiency of, response to catastrophe claim, Cyclone Tracy (1974), 87–9
   unity, 89; loyalty, 104
   remuneration, 104; competance, 107
   leader, international reinsurance market, 89, 91, 92, 94, 102–4
   seeks information, 89, 100
   expansion, restructuring, recruitment, 90–2, 96–109
      overseas offices and contracts;
         United States, 91
         Australia, 91, 102
         Spain, 91, 103
         Latin America, 81, 91, 102
         Japan, 91, 92, 102
         Singapore, 91
         France, 103
         New Zealand, 102
         Germany, 103
         Scandinavia, 103
         Commonwealth, 81
         see also individual company entries
   survives takeover bid, 91
   international stature and reputation, 85, 87, 89–91, 92, 102, 104, 109
   on Lloyd's Council, 92, *93*
   catastrophe, claims, 87, 94

   losses collected by, 87, 94, *102*
   company accounts, 1974–94, *90*, 91, *102*
   service to clients, 96–109
   market position, *90*, 91, 94, *102*
   pioneering research, *63*, 97–8, *99*, 102–3
      Geographic Analysis Project (GAP), 97–8, *99*, 107
   pride in, 107
   reinsurance prospects;
      China, 103
      Europe, 103
      overseas, 107
   professionalism, 96–109
   cohesion, 104
   innovation, 98–9, 102, 106–7
   qualitative change, 103
   financial resources, *90*, 103–4
   independence and objectivity, 104, 107
   ethics and principles, 83, 106–7
   future prospects, 102–9
   Group Board portrait, *106*
Greig, George, burgher of Kirkcaldy, near Edinburgh, tallow chandler, married daughter of John Archer, 8–9
Greig, John (born 1745), clerk of Leslie and Edinburgh, married Agnes Sibbald, 9
Greig, John (son of John Greig, above) held Militia Insurance Policy, *9*, 9–10
Greig, John Andrew, 10, 11
   family, 11, *11*, 105
   portrait, *11*
   manager at Sun Life, 11–12, 13
   chairs dinner, *13*
   cables son Walter, 19
Greig, John S., Chairman, Greig Fester Group, son of Walter and Mildred Greig;
   vexed by W.T. Greig Ltd wartime evacuation, 57, 70
   joins W.T. Greig Ltd, 1950, 70–1
   responsible efficiency of Latin American account, 70–1
   diplomat and linguist, 70
   travels, 70–1; recreation, 70
   interviews Peter Keats, 73
      transfers Latin American reinsurance account to, 73, *74*
   concentrates on London office, 74
   decides company needs new approach, 80, 104
   appoints management consultants, 80
   considers buying broking house, 81
   promotes staff seminars, 81

INDEX

attends Oxford Centre for Management
 Studies, 81, *100*
 meets Desmond Graves at, 81
 considers merger, Fester, Fothergill & Hartung,
 81–3
 promotes magnanimous approach to, 82–3
 announces foundation, Greig Fester, 83
 honours father in death, 84–5
 applauds unity of staff, Cyclone Tracy relief, 89
 oversees expansion and recruitment, 90–2, 104
 sets up W.T. Greig (South Africa), 91
 elected to Council of Lloyd's, 1986, 92
  offers to resign from, 92
  re-elected, 92
  elected Deputy Chairman of, 92, *93*
  responsibility for training, regulation and
   Lloyd's affairs, 92
 reinsurance, future of, 104, 106–7
 portraits, *74, 93, 105*
Greig, Kenneth, eldest son of John Andrew
 Greig, 7, *11*
 school, 17
 employed Sun Life, 13, 22
 in uniform of London Scottish territorials, *18*
 Great War service in France, 7, 18, 39, 85
 news of from France, 19
 Partner, W.T. Greig Ltd, 6–8
 letter from brother Walter, 45
 cables Walter with good news, 53
 dies, 1960, 84
Greig, Leonard, third son of John Andrew Greig, *11*
 school, 17
 employed Sun Fire, 13, 22
 in uniform of London Scottish territorials, *18*
 Great War service, 7, 18, 39, 85
 news of from France, 19
 wartime disability, 7, 22, 38
 Partner, W.T. Greig Ltd, 6, 8, 24, 39
  runs direct insurance section at, 38
 at Carlton Club, 55
 attends office in old age, 84
 dies, 84
Greig, Mildred née Rowe, wife of Walter Greig;
 joins W.T. Greig Ltd, 38, *38*
 family history, 38
 marriage and honeymoon, 39–46
 companionship, 40
 at Kingswood, 57
 dies, 84
Greig, Roy, youngest son of John Andrew Greig,
 11, *11*

Great War Service, killed in action, 28 March
 1918, 7, 22
Greig, Thomas, son of John Greig (born 1745),
 printer, 9
 married Rebecca Clunie, 10
Greig, Walter T., second son of John Andrew
 Greig, 7, *11*
 history of family, *11*, 6–9, 11, 13; school, 17
 early employment with Royal Exchange
  Assurance;
  London, 13–15
  appointed Manager, Buenos Aires
   branch, 7, 15–17
  promoted in London, 19–21
 linguist, 17, 20, 70
 recreation, 15, 17
 letters to Ferrers Daniell, 17–19
 business philosophy, 14, 107
 business acumen, 14, 17, 36–7, 41–3, 50, 61, 63,
  80, 84–5
 in uniform of London Scottish territorials, *18*
 volunteers, Great War, 18–19
 exempted from military service, 19
 honoured by associates, *16*, 49
 founds W.T. Greig Ltd, 6–8, 21–2, 24, 36–8
  motive, 21–2, 85
 develops reciprocal reinsurance business, 21,
  24, 36–45, 48, 51, 53, 61, 63
 excess of loss reinsurance policies, 33
 marries Mildred Rowe, 36, 38, *38*, 39
 honeymoon, mixes business with pleasure, 39,
  41–6
 travel notebooks, *37*, 40, 50, 68
 optimism and expansion, 48
 develops concept of agricultural all-risks cover,
  48
 interviews Cuthbert Heath of Lloyd's,
  49, 51
 pessimism and contraction, 49, 51
 receives good news, 53
 good fortune, 53
 the 'Traveller', 20, 40, 50, 51, 61, 68
 Kingswood home, 57, *57*
 World War II evacuation, 55, 57, *57*
 hands over reins of company, 61
 negotiates with Perón regime, 62–3, 85
 portraits, *62*, 11
 supports merger, 84
 attends company in old age, 84
 dies, 84; family affection, 84–5
 character, 14–22, 37, 80, 84–5, 107

121

see also Douglas Rathbone; W.T. Greig Ltd; Mildred Greig; John S. Greig

Grieg, Edvard, composer, 8

Guardian Assurance, 'morning after' view from office during London blitz, *60*

market leader in any one risk cover reinsurance, 67

Hall, Geoffrey, Greig Fester Claims Manager, facilitates catastrophe relief, Darwin, Cyclone Tracy, 87–8

Hamburg, Mund & Fester office at (1876), 28

Hartung, Carl, former manager, Russian Imperial Fire Office, founds Hartung partnership in London, 26, 28

Hartung, Carl Frederic, son of Frederick Hartung, Partner, Fester, Fothergill & Hartung, 54

Hartung, Frederick, brother and Partner of Carl Hartung, 26

travelled widely, 28

later Partner, Fester, Fothergill & Hartung, 54

Hashimoto, Tamotsu, President, Toa Re, Japan, befriends John Merison and Geoffrey Hudson, 74, 76

contemplates treaty with W.T. Greig Ltd, 77

Havana, *35, 51*; business call on Greig's honeymoon, 41

insurance risks, 41

Hawkshaw, Sir John, docks engineer, Buenos Aires, 15, 17

Heath, Cuthbert, of Lloyd's, innovator;
compiled 'earthquake book' for assessing cover, 63–4

evolved principle of 'excess of loss' reinsurance, 48–9

interviewed, regarding agricultural 'all risks' cover, 49

airline passenger policies, 51

Heckscher, Martin of St Petersburg, reinsurance broker, associate of Frederick Hartung, 26, 28

Herne Bay, Greig family photographed at, *11*

flood threat to, *99*

Hiles, Edward, Fire Manager, Royal Exchange, doubled company's overseas business, 13–14, 17

Hill, Bill, Greig Fester Director, formerly of W.T. Greig Ltd and Fester, Fothergill & Hartung;

analyses company strength, 82

notes merger magnanimity, 83–4

Hitchman, Frank, Greig Fester Group Board member, 1990– , *106*

HMS *Indefatigable*, wartime command, Douglas Rathbone, 58; served in also by Peter Keats, 73

Hodge, Percy, Secretary of the Royal Exchange, 20

promotes Walter Greig, Assistant Fire Manager, 20–1

letters from, 20–1

Hoorda, Greg, Greig Fester staff, Sydney, facilitates catastrophe relief, Darwin, Cyclone Tracy, 87–9

HRM Queen Elizabeth II;

visits Adelaide after 1954 earthquake, 65

opens Lloyd's new premises, 1986, 92

Hudson, Geoffrey, formerly of Norwich Union, captured Singapore, imprisoned Changi; later Tokyo head, British Insurance Group; promoted Japanese insurance industry; Eastern Manager, Mercantile & General; Tokyo adviser, W.T. Greig Ltd, 76

Hurlingham Club, Buenos Aires, 15, 17

Hurricane Betsy, Miami, 1965, *85*

formative reinsurance catastrophe; damage and cost; Lloyd's loss, effect on reinsurance market, 86

Hurricane Hugo, USA, 1989, reinsurance cost, 94, *102*

IMAR (Instituto Mixto Argentino de Reaseguros), Argentina;

nationalised reinsurance company, 61, 63

Walter Greig negotiates fire treaty with, 63

see also INDER

Imperial Fire Office, Russia, Carl Hartung manager for, 26

INDER (Instituto Nacional de Reaseguros), Argentina, formerly IMAR, government monopolised reinsurance company, W.T. Greig Ltd fire treaty with, 63

Jakor Insurance Company of Russia;

Carl Hartung sets up London agency for, 26, 28

Keats, Peter, Greig Fester Group Board Director, *106*

formerly of C.E. Golding & Co. and Munich Re, 73

joined W.T. Greig Ltd 1963, 73

travels to 'earthquake countries', 74

portrait, *74, 106*

Latin American operations, 74

INDEX

lauds Devon House premises, 96
Kiln Syndicate, Colin Murray, underwriter for, 88
Kingswood, Surrey;
   Walter and Mildred Greig's home, 57, *57*
   evacuation premises of Greigs, 1939–41, 57
Kobe earthquake, 1995, *108*, 109
Kristeller, John, established W.T. Greig (South Africa) (1961), 91
Kyodo (Japan), client, Fester, Fothergill & Hartung, 55, 71
Kyoei Mutual (Japan), client, Fester, Fothergill & Hartung, 71
   Harry Farmer negotiates fire treaty with, 71

Labour Government, effects of 1945 landslide election, 60
La Buenos Aires (Argentina), client, W.T. Greig Ltd, 21, 37
Lainston House, management seminars held at, *100*
La Metropolitana (Cuba), fire treaty with W.T. Greig Ltd, 37, 41
La Préservatrice (France), motor insurance treaty with Fester, Fothergill & Hartung, 71
La Providence (France), motor insurance treaty with Fester, Fothergill & Hartung, 71
La Rosario (Argentina), client, W.T. Greig Ltd, 21, 37, 53
   fire treaty, 38
   cables from, 50
   office, *47*
   agricultural all risks scheme, 48–9
   air route policies, 51
Laurence Pountney Lane, premises, Fester, Fothergill & Hartung, 1910–24, 8, 54
Leng Roberts, Anglo-Argentine finance house;
   R.W. Roberts, Walter Greig associate from, 17
   Walter Greig promised business from, 21
   associates from honour Walter Greig, *49*
Lime Street office, first premises, Greig Fester, 88
Liverpool Underwriters Association, Old Exchange Rooms, financial power of, 29–30
Lloyd's of London;
   early reinsurance policy, 24, 37; practice, 14, 24, 29
   subscription room, 29, *29*
   accredits Fester, Fothergill & Hartung (1910), 54
   reciprocal treaties, 37
   inter-war policy, 48–9
   prestige as marine insurer, 48; reputation, 48
   Cuthbert Heath of, 48, 63–4
   post-war underwriting practice, 88
   formalities, 55
   'earthquake book', 63–4
   earthquake and windstorm reinsurance rates, 64
   catastrophe cover, 64, 65
   accredits W.T. Greig Ltd (1963), 73, 85
   losses and recovery, Hurricane Betsy (1965), 86
   syndicates affected, Cyclone Tracy (1974), 87, 88
   appoints committee, Cyclone Tracy relief, 88
   elects John S. Greig to Council (1986), 92, *93*
   HRM Queen Elizabeth II opens new premises (1986), 92
   elects John S. Greig, Deputy Chairman (1991), 92, *93*, 94
   Council of Lloyd's (1991), *93*
   Sir Patrick Neill's report, 92
   'problems and scandals', 92
   market crisis and losses, 94
   brokers and syndicates, the future, 104, 106–7
London Bridge, 'morning after' view, London blitz, *60*
London & Lancashire, client, Fester, Fothergill & Hartung, disassociate 1959, 30, 71–2
London Scottish Territorials (Regiment);
   Greig brothers volunteer in, 18, *18*
   at Western Front, 19
   James Galbraith, sergeant-cook of, 39
London Treaty, mentioned in negotiations, Walter Greig and National Insurance Co. of New Zealand, 43
Losse, Dieter, Greig Fester Group Deputy Chairman, Chief Executive and Board member, *106*
   linguist, 73
   portrait, *73*
   specialist, Far East operations, 74, 76–7
   on W.T. Greig Ltd, reputation, 80
   on overseas expansion, 91–2
   promotes added-value service, 97, 100
   commitment of, 103
   on Greig Fester Group, 103–4
   on future role of reinsurance broking, 97, 103–4

MacArthur, General Douglas, allows rebuilding Japan's post-war insurance industry, 76
malicious damage, rate enquiry for bomb threat, 50
Mallard, Mr, General Manager, National Mortgage and Agency Company, New Zealand;

resists reciprocal treaty with W.T. Greig Ltd, 40
   over-ruled by Board, 44
   entertains Walter and Mildred Greig, 43
Manners and Miller (Edinburgh), booksellers, employers of John Greig, 9, 10
marine, reinsurance, historical importance of, 24
   insurance claims, 39
   Lloyd's turn to non-marine, 48
   cargo reinsurance, W.T. Greig Ltd excess of loss contract, 61
   risks, ceded to IMAR (Argentina), 63
   insurance premiums increase, supertankers, 86
   exposure, reports required, 100
   passengers, liability for, 102
MBM Re (France), Greig Fester acquisition, 91
Menzie, Mr, Commercial of Australia, enquires rate, Walter Greig, insuring against malicious damage, 50
Mercantile & General;
   Robin Snook's former employer, 76
   Geoffrey Hudson, Eastern Manager (Japan) of, 76
Merison, John ('Hurricane John'), Director, W.T. Greig Ltd, foreign sales, 73
   portrait, *73*
   Far East travels, 74; specialist Japan, 74, 76–7
   leading director, 81
   secures client, Toa Re, 89–90
   recommends merger, 81
   magnanimity of, 84
Miami, Florida, Hurricane Betsy (1965), *85*
Militia Act of 1802, Scottish conscription law, *9*, 10
Mitchell, Andrew, Greig Fester UK division, demonstrates Geographic Analysis Project, 98
Mores, the Revd Edward, first calculated mathematical principles, life assurance, 7
motor, garage and car premiums, Havana (1926), 41
   insurance cover, Fester, Fothergill & Hartung contract, 71
Mund & Fester (Antwerp, Hamburg, Liverpool);
   founded, *27*, 28, *28*
   merger, Fester, Fothergill & Hartung founded 1909, 30
Mund, Adolph, founder Mund & Fester, Antwerp (1874), *27*, 30
Mund, Fester & Fothergill (Liverpool), merger, Fester, Fothergill & Hartung (London), *54*
Mund, Fester & Hartung (London), founded (1896), 28

   Liverpool branch, 30; represents Swiss Re, *30*
   Fester, Fothergill & Hartung, founded (1909), *54*
Munich Re, founded 1880, 25
   Peter Keats at, 73
Murphy, Jean, Kenneth Greig's daughter, recalls affinity of Greig brothers, 84
Murray, Colin, underwriter, Kiln Syndicate, chairs Lloyd's Cyclone Tracy committee, 88

National Insurance Company of New Zealand; client, W.T. Greig Ltd, 39, 49
   profit and loss, 49
   discusses reciprocal reinsurance with, 43, *43*
   negotiates 'any one risk' treaty, 67
National Mortgage and Agency Company (New Zealand), James Galbraith's employer, 39
Neill, Sir Patrick, Chairman, committee on Lloyd's market, recommends end, 'insider' control, 92
New Rotterdam Insurance Company, client, W.T. Greig Ltd, catastrophe risk treaty, 64
Nicholas Lane (London);
   W.T. Greig Ltd first office, 6, *6*, 13, 22, 36, 104
   insurance history, 7–8, 26, 54
Nissan (Japan), client, Fester, Fothergill & Hartung, 55, 71
No. 14 Cornhill, W.T. Greig Ltd post-war premises, 57
Northern Insurance Co., client, Fester, Fothergill & Hartung, catastrophe reinsurance treaty, 64, 67, 72–3
Norwich Union, client, Fester, Fothergill & Hartung, 64
   Geoffrey Hudson's former employer, 74, 76

Old Exchange Rooms, premises, Liverpool Underwriters Association, 29, *29*
Ordnance Survey, encourage Greig Fester to develop Geographic Analysis Project, 98
Orvieto, Greig honeymoon cruise liner, passage home, 45
Oxford Centre for Management Studies (Templeton College), John S. Greig attends management course, 81

Panama Canal, route of Walter and Mildred Greig's honeymoon voyage, 40, *41*
Park, James, Lincoln's Inn lawyer, notes importance of marine reinsurance, 24
Perón Regime, Argentina, nationalises reinsurance market, 61, 63

INDEX

John S. Greig experiences, 70
   recalls father's negotiations with, 85
Phoenix (London), reciprocal treaty with the
   Sun, 25
Place Verte 33, Antwerp, Heinrich Fester's
   business premises, 28
Putney Heath (London), Greig family home at, 11
   Greig brothers at school at, 17

Queensland of Australia, client, fire treaty,
   W.T. Greig Ltd, 38

Rathbone, Douglas;
   school, 50
   joins W.T. Greig Ltd (1928), 14, 36, 50, *50*
   accounts clerk, reinsurance, 50
   decodes cables, 50
   officer, HMS *Indefatigable*, 58
   at Okinawa, battle, 58
   meets Greig clients, Australasia 58
   travels, 61
   makes first air journey of W.T. Greig Ltd staff, 61
   Director, W.T. Greig Ltd (1948), 61
   runs accounts and administration, 80
   business acumen, 61, 64, 66, 68
   the 'Inventor', 66–8, 70
   marine cargo contract, 61
   devises concept, 'any one risk' cover policies,
      66–7
      annual aggregate bushfire clause, 67–8
   develops catastrophe reinsurance business, 64
   leading director, 81
   'guiding hand', 50
   'moulds' company, 68, 70
   holds 'reins of company', 61
   opinion, on Walter Greig, 14, 36
      W.T. Greig Ltd, 36, 55
      1932 results, 53
      reinsurance policy, Australasia, 46
   portraits, *50, 69*
Rectory House, Southwark Bridge, London,
   premises, Fester, Fothergill & Hartung, 55
Regis House, London, Greig Fester's head office,
   60, *79*, 96
reinsurance;
   principles, 14, 32–3, 36–7, 111
   importance of, 14, 30, 32–3, 100, 104, 106–7, 109
   historical origins, 24–6, 28–31, 37, 48, 60
   practice and administration, 14, 32–3, 36, 46,
      50, 57, 66–7, 80, 86–92, 94, 96–109
   brokers, 26, 55, 73, 80, 86, 92, 94, 96, 103, 104

   new role, 98, 100
   commission, 32–3, 37, 38, 44, 45, 46, 49, 51, 53,
      64, 71, 91, 97
   policy, treaties and contracts;
      fire, 14, 32, 37, 53, 63, 71, 72
      marine, 24, 39, 48, 63, 86, 100
         cargo, 61; passengers, 102
      construction, 32, 41, 50, 86, 87–8, 94, 98–9, 109
      motor, 41, 71
      airlines, 50–1, 86
      malicious damage, 50
      domestic mortgage, 97
      reciprocal, 25, 36, 46, 49, 51, 53, 61, 63–5, 71,
         74
      facultative, 32, 37, 46, 55
      proportional, 32, 65
      quota-share, 32
      surplus, 32, 66, 67
      catastrophe, 33, 49, 56, 63–5, 67–8, 73, 76,
         86–88, 90, 94, 97, 98–100, 102–3, 106–7
      premiums, 13, 14, 25, 64, 85, 97
      claims, 25, 49, 68, 73, 86–9, 94, *102*
      retrocession market, 94
      futures market, 106
      see also catastrophes; earthquake; fire;
         flood; subsidence; wheat-rust;
         windstorm
   'any one event', 33, 68
   'any one risk', 66, 67, 68, 74, 86
   'excess of loss', 33, 49, 61, 73, 97, 100, 109
   (agricultural) 'all risks', 48, 49
   'annual aggregate' (bushfire clause), 68
   shadow, 57
   'block' settlements, 88
   'stop-loss' cover, 100
international business;
   risk, 18, 29, 32, 61, 84, 89, 100, 102
   expenditure, 100, 102
   contraction and loss;
      Great War, 25
      Slump, 49, 51
      World War II, 57–8, 76
      post-war, 85, 86, 92, 94, 97
      nationalisation, Argentina, 61, 63
   expansion and profit, 13–5, 53, 60–1, 64, 67,
      85–6, *90*, 91
Fester, Fothergill & Hartung, 26, 30, 54–8, 64,
   71–3, 81–4, 102
W.T. Greig Ltd, 21, 24, 30, 36–46, 48–9, 51, 53,
   55, 57–8, 61, 63–8, 70–1, 73–4, 76–7, 80–4,
   86, 89–90

Greig Fester, 87–92, 94, 97–8, 100–9
   innovation, 97–8, *99*, 100, 102–3, 104, 106–7, 109
   future, 100, 102–4, 106–7, 109
   see also John S. Greig; Lloyd's
Remuera, Greig honeymoon cruise liner, 41, 42
Ritchie, George, Chairman, National Insurance Co. of New Zealand;
   wishes to discuss reciprocal reinsurance with Walter Greig, 39–40
   secures treaty with W.T. Greig Ltd, 42–4
RMS *Orcoma*, Greig's outward sailing honeymoon cruise liner, 40, *40*
Roberts, R.W. (Bobbie) of Leng Roberts, friend of Walter Greig, Buenos Aires, 17
   promises business to W.T. Greig Ltd, 21, 24
   takes airline policy, 51
Robinson, Denys, originally of Fester, Fothergill & Hartung, Latin American account, 70
Rowe, Mildred, *see* Mildred Greig
Rowe, Thomas of Weymouth, Dorset, father of Mildred Rowe, family history, 38
Royal (UK), early assurance company, 30
   takes over London & Lancashire, 71–2
   losses, 73
Royal Exchange Assurance Corporation (UK), early assurance company, 6, 13
   early history of, 13–15, 26
   see also Walter T. Greig
Royal Exchange Avenue, premises, W.T. Greig Ltd (1926–39), 48

Samarang Company of Indonesia, Walter Greig cancels treaty with, 44
sawmill, classic reinsurance hazard, 32
Scott, Smith and Stein, bankers, Edinburgh, John Greig's employers, 9
Sedgwick, London's largest broking company, 89
   attempts takeover of Greig Fester, 1982, 91
Selhurst Grammar School, Douglas Rathbone attended, 50
Sentrakas (South Africa), agricultural co-operative insurer, client, W.T. Greig (South Africa), 91
Shepherd, Elspeth (née Greig), Walter and Mildred Greig's daughter;
   recalls father regretted not learning French at school, 17
   notes parents' affinity, 39
   recalls wartime evacuation of W.T. Greig Ltd, 57
   speaks affectionately of father, 84
Shoenfield, Meryl, Walter Greig's niece, daughter of Lilias Green (née Greig), explains reason Walter Greig founded his company, 85
Sibbald, Agnes of Edinburgh, wife of John Greig, 9
Sievwright & Greig (Edinburgh), sign John Greig's Militia Insurance Policy, 9–10, *10*
Simmonds, Michael, Greig Fester Group Board member 1990– , *106*
   finance director, W.T. Greig Ltd, 82
   on W.T. Greig Ltd accounts, 82
   portrait, *82*
Simpson, Barry, of Wellington, New Zealand, Manager, National Insurance Company, discusses city insurance with Walter Greig, 45
the Slump, effects on insurance market, 49, 51
   fraudulent claims during, 51
Snook, Robin, formerly of Mercantile & General, comments on Geoffrey Hudson, 76
South British, Walter Greig meets Percy Upton of, 42
Spiller, David, Chief Executive, Greig Fester International Ltd;
   opinion on future of broking, 98, 100
   potential for reinsurance, China, 103
   links with Scandinavia, 103
St Katharine's Dock (London), location of Devon House, *95, 96, 96*
Standard Marine (Liverpool), early assurance company, 30
Sterling Offices of Lloyd's, reinsurance brokers, 37
Storebrand Company of Norway (1860s), reciprocal fire treaty with Phoenix, 25
Suffolk House, Laurence Pountney Lane, London, premises, Fester, Fothergill & Hartung, 1910–24, 54
subsidence (UK, 1986), problem claims, 97
Sun Fire, parent company, Sun Life, 13
Sun Life Assurance (London);
   John Andrew Greig, manager of, 11; office, *12*, 13
   son worked for, 11, 13
Supple, Barry, historian of Royal Exchange Assurance, explains international strength of, 14
Swiss Re (Compagnie Suisse de Réassurances of Zurich), *38*
   Dieter Losse's former employer, 73
Sydney, Australia, bushfires, *101*

INDEX

Thames estuary, flood prognosis, GAP, 99
Thomson, Annie of Ross-shire, wife, Thomas Greig, 10
The Times, letter in, 7
   avidly read by Greig brothers, 36, 55
   comment on Australian catastrophes, 65
Toa Fire and Marine Reinsurance Company (Toa Re);
   post-war restructuring, 76
   client, W.T. Greig Ltd, 90
Tokyo 'zone five' earthquake catastrophe risk, 76–7
   1923 earthquake, *56*
Toplis and Harding, Robert Cole's employer, 88
Trading with the Enemy Act, wartime legislation against trade with enemy powers, 57
Treaty Re (London), early reinsurance company, 26
Trebilcock, Clive, historian of Phoenix Reinsurance Company, notes leading role of, 25

Union (of Paris), offers fire treaty to Royal Exchange, 26
Union Insurance Company (USA), earliest recorded reinsurance treaty, 24
Union Marine (Liverpool), early reinsurance company, 30
Unión Nacional, mentioned in cable, Walter Greig, 53
United (Australia), client, W.T. Greig Ltd, 66
   seeks reciprocal business with Walter Greig, 45–6
   profit and loss, 49
   marine cargo excess of loss contract, 61
Upton, Percy, of South British, meets Walter Greig in Auckland, 42

Valdera, Greig honeymoon cruise liner, 45, 48
Victory Re (London), early reinsurance company, 26

W.T. Greig (Australia), founded 1957, 'bright jewel in Greig crown', 71, 91
W.T. Greig (South Africa), founded 1961, 91
W.T. Greig Ltd;
   founded (1921), 6-7, 21, 24–5, 33
   directors, 7–8, 22; emoluments, 38
   character of company, 82
   reinsurance policy, 14, 21, 24, 45, 68, 73, 80
      reciprocal reinsurance treaties, 36–39, 44–5, 49, 51, 53, 58, 61, 64–5, 74, 90
   'excess of loss' policies, 33, 61
   agricultural 'all-risks' cover, 48-9
   'all-risk' contracts, 51
   fire treaties, 37–8, 53, 63, 67
   facultative reinsurance, 55
   earthquake reinsurance, leader in, 63, 74, 76-8
   catastrophe reinsurance, 64–5, 67–8, 74, 76–7, 86, 90
      rates, 64
   proportional treaties, 65
   pioneers, 'any one risk' policies, 66–7, 68, 74, 86
      'any one event' policies, 68
      'annual aggregate' bushfire clause, 68
   premises;
      No. 34 Nicholas Lane (1921), 7–8
      Royal Exchange Avenue (1926), 48
      No. 14, Cornhill (1942), 57
   early fortunes, 36–8
   inter-war optimism and growth, 48
   recruitment and expansion, 46, 48
   profits, 37, 38, 46, 48, 49, 51, 55
      see also Lloyd's
   communication problems, 50
   office life, 50, 55
   inter-war pessimism and contraction, 49–51
   the Slump, effect of, 49, 55; fraudulent claims, 51
   good fortune, 53
   pre-war stagnation, 55
   wartime evacuation (1939–41), 55, 57, *57*
   World War II, impact on business, 57, 58
   post-war growth, 61, 63, 64
   contracts;
      marine cargo, 55, 61
      INDER (Argentina), 61–3
      Latin America, 81
      Japan, 81–89
      Toa Re, 74, 76–7, 90
      Commonwealth, 81
      Australia, 86, 87
      see also individual company entries
   pioneering and innovative company, 66, 68, 70, 80
   developmental phases, 68
   restructuring and recruitment, 70, 73
   accredited, Lloyd's, 1963, 73, 85
   income analysis, *75*, 91
   expansion and rationalisation, 80–1
   world reinsurance leader, 77, 80
   good reputation, 76–7, 80

explores buying broking house, 81
appoints management consultants, 80
proposes merger, Fester, Fothergill & Hartung, 81
merger talks, 83; difficulties, 82
considerations, 82–3; merger announcement, 83
Greig Fester founded (1974), 83
see also Greig Fester; Kenneth Greig; Leonard Greig; Walter T. Greig; Peter Keats; Dieter Losse; John Merison; Douglas Rathbone; R.W. Roberts
Walker, John of Edinburgh, printing partner of Thomas Greig, 9
Wallas, Brian, Partner, Fester, Fothergill & Hartung;
recruited, 1950, 72
portrait, *72*
Japan specialist, 74
with Frank Gill negotiated breakthrough contract with the Royal, 73
recommends merger, 82
consideration for staff, 83
Greig Fester Group Board member, *106*
Waters, Steve, Greig Fester Claims Officer, facilitates catastrophe relief, Darwin, Cyclone Tracy, 87
Wellington, 'hazardous town', Walter Greig visits, 45
West of Scotland Company, active early reciprocal reinsurance company, 25
Wetherley, Reg, underwriter, Northern, discusses catastrophe reinsurance with Douglas Rathbone, 64
wheat-rust, Argentina, drought harvest plague claims, effects on W.T. Greig Ltd premiums, 49
Whitlam, Gough, Prime Minister of Australia, 1974, 86
Williams, Jack, General Manager, United of Sydney, client, W.T. Greig Ltd, accepts first any one risk policy, 66

windstorm;
premiums, Lloyd's, 64
Greig Fester, 97, 98
exposure, 98
cover, 68
losses, 86, 88–9, 94, 97, *102*
damage and cost, Queensland (1954), 65
Hurricane Betsy (1965), *85*, 86
Cyclone Tracy (1974), 86, *86*; relief, 87–9
CAT87J (1987), 33, *33*, 94, 97, *102*
Hurricane Hugo (1989), 94, *102*
Europe (1990), 94, 97, *102*
Sydney (1990), *102*
Japan typhoon (1990), *102*
Hurricane Andrew (1992), *102*
Hurricane Gilbert (1988), *102*
risk;
Jamaica, 64
Manhattan, 94
Japan, 102
Australia, 102
research;
Australia, 102–3
GAP (UK), 97–8, *99*, 106
see also catastrophes; reinsurance
World War I, *see* Great War
World War II;
Blitz, *55*
reinsurance market during, 57–8, 71
W.T. Greig Ltd during, 55, 57, *57*, 58
Fester, Fothergill & Hartung during, 57
effects of, 57
post-war developments, 60–1, 71, 76

Yamada, Seiji, Managing Director, Toa Re; later W.T. Greig Ltd's senior representative, Tokyo, 77, 92
comment, W.T. Greig Ltd's entry, Japanese market, 90

Location	
LONDON	■
PARIS	■
NEW YORK CITY	■
PHILADELPHIA	■
MADRID	■
MEXICO CITY	■
LIMA	●
SANTIAGO	●

■ PRINCIPAL OFFICES